MODELS OF LANGUAGE
DEVELOPMENT

MODELS OF LANGUAGE DEVELOPMENT

Rosemary J. Stevenson

Department of Psychology
University of Durham

OPEN UNIVERSITY PRESS
Milton Keynes · Philadelphia

Open University Press
Open University Educational Enterprises Limited
12 Cofferidge Close
Stony Stratford
Milton Keynes MK11 1BY

and
242 Cherry Street
Philadelphia, PA 19106, USA

First Published 1988

British Library Cataloguing in Publication Data

Stevenson, Rosemary J.
    Theoretical issues in language development.
    1. Children. Language skills. Acquisition.
    Psychological aspects
    I. Title
    401'.9

    ISBN 0-335-09521-6
    ISBN 0-335-09520-8 Pbk

Library of Congress Cataloging-in-Publication Data

Stevenson, Rosemary.
        Theoretical issues in language development / Rosemary Stevenson.
            p.   cm.
        Bibliography: p.
        Includes index.
        ISBN 0-335-09521-6   ISBN 0-335-09520-8 (pbk.)
        1. Language acquisition.   2. Competence and performance
    (Linguistics)   3. Government-binding theory (Linguistics)
    I. Title.
    P118.S74 1988
    401'.9—dc19   88-19659   CIP

Typeset by Colset Private Limited, Singapore
Printed in Great Britain by J.W. Arrowsmith Limited, Bristol

Contents

Preface

I first thought I would write a book on language development in 1981. In that year, I presented a talk to the Developmental Section of the British Psychological Society in which I was critical of the current models of language development. After that talk, I felt dissatisfied. It is one thing to be critical but quite another to be constructive. This book represents my attempts to expunge those dissatisfactions and find a constructive solution to the problem of language development.

In 1983, I was lucky enough to spend a year in the United States, six months at the University of Massachusetts at Amherst, and six months at the University of Texas at Austin. While I was there I took the opportunity to sit in on some graduate courses in linguistics. I was very fortunate in both Amherst and Austin. At Amherst, the syntax class was taught by Edwin Williams and the semantics class by Barbara Partee. Both of them nurtured my interest in linguistics and introduced me to the intricacies of Chomsky's latest work.

At Austin, the syntax class was taught by Lee Baker and the semantics class by Irena Heim. Both consolidated my interest and my expertise in linguistics. I was particularly lucky here because Lee Baker's paper in *Linguistic Inquiry* in 1979 had been the first to spark my interest in the issue of learnability. I am very grateful for his support and encouragement while I was in Texas.

Needless to say, there are many people I should acknowledge. The first is David, who put up with me during the writing. Second are my cognitive science students of the last two years who have suffered, seemingly cheerfully, various versions of this book in their lectures. A number of other people have contributed time, comments and ideas. These include Hazel Emslie, Ros Crawley, Kerry Sims, Marion England, Kate Gillen and Margaret Hall. I also acknowledge the Cognitive Science Program at the University of Massachusetts where I spent a stimulating six months talking about language development and many other aspects of language, and the Center for Cognitive Science and the Sloan Foundation for providing me with facilities and ambience for my thoughts on the book to take shape. Finally, my thanks to my colleagues at Durham who have to put up with me when I am not on sabbatical and who have over the years heard and contributed to my ideas on the development of language.

CHAPTER 1

Language and Language Development

What is acquired?

An adult model of language use involves more than just a knowledge of language. It also involves aspects of general cognition or non-linguistic world knowledge, and aspects of social knowledge. We will start our discussion of language development by giving some examples of adult usage which will set the scene for looking at how children develop language. The view that I will take in this book is that adults bring to bear a number of different knowledge sources when using language and that these different knowledge sources can be regarded as distinct, even though they must interact in some way during language use.

For purposes of discussion, I will concentrate here on referring expressions (e.g. *the man*, *he*, *it*) and the kinds of problems they pose for language understanding. In particular I will consider pronouns because they provide an ideal example of the way in which language comprehension depends upon different sources of information, both linguistic and non-linguistic. I will briefly illustrate the way in which we can use four different knowledge sources to interpret pronouns. I will begin each of the following sections with a sentence that will be used to illustrate the use of these different knowledge sources.

Syntax

John said that Bill liked him.

In this example, in principle, if there were no grammar, then the pronoun *him* could refer to either John or Bill. However, this is not the case. There is a syntactic constraint on pronominal interpretation that rules out *Bill* as a permissible antecedent. Briefly, this constraint is that a non-reflexive pronoun, like *him*, cannot have an antecedent in the same clause. So that is an example of how syntactic knowledge can contribute to the comprehension of *him* in this sentence.

Semantics

A man came in. He was very wet.

In this example, the pronoun *he* is normally taken to refer to the man. However, there is nothing in the syntax of the sentence that could contribute to this interpretation. It is only by means of semantic knowledge – something akin to a model of the situation described by the two sentences – that the pronoun *he* can be assigned to the antecedent, *a man*. So this is where semantics can help. That is, on encountering the words *a man*, we can set up an entity to stand for the man in a discourse model. Then, on encountering the pronoun, this acts as an instruction to look for an entity in the model which agrees with the pronoun in number and gender. In this example, there is only one entity in the model (the man) so the pronoun can be assigned to that entity. This is only a very informal account of the semantics involved. More formal models have been developed in philosophy by Kamp (1984), in linguistics by Heim (1983), in artificial intelligence by Webber (1979) and in psychology by Johnson-Laird (1983) and by Stenning (1978).

Pragmatics (non-linguistic knowledge)

Jane was late for her appointment with Sue and she hurried to get a taxi.

In this example, neither syntax nor semantics can identify the antecedent of the pronoun *she*. The pronoun is contained in a separate clause from the one containing the two potential antecedents (*Jane* and *Sue*). This means that on syntactic grounds both potential antecedents are available. Similarly, a semantic analysis of the sentences will not help much either. The pronoun *she* is a particular number and gender, and

both number and gender are compatible with either of the two antecedents. So semantics cannot rule out either of the two potential antecedents for us. For example, let us assume that we have built up an
internal discourse model of the events described in the sentence; more
specifically, we have derived a representation of the first clause and are
in the process of interpreting the second clause. Then if we interpret *she*
as either Jane or Sue, both of those interpretations could be true in the
discourse model that we have developed so far. So semantics cannot
help us in this sentence.

However, there is a sense in which the sentence is not truly ambiguous. This is because we can make inferences from general
knowledge about the likely consequences of someone being late for an
appointment to infer that *she*, in fact, refers to Jane. Of course, we
could interpret the pronoun as referring to Sue, but the resulting interpretation would describe a much less likely event. The inference that
she refers to Jane is a plausible inference rather than a necessary one.
That is what we mean by pragmatics.

Social knowledge

In considering social knowledge I will turn from pronouns to determiner phrases. Determiners are words like *a* and *the*, and they occur in
determiner phrases, such as *a man* or *the man*. As Roger Brown pointed
out in 1958, an individual can have many different names. For example,
the four-legged noisy thing that shares my house with me can be called
an animal, a dog, a spaniel, or Spot. How I refer to this creature will
depend on what I assume the listener knows. If I assume that we share
the knowledge of my dog, I will refer to her as *Spot*. But if I assume the
listener does not know I have a dog, I will refer to her as *my dog*. It is my
judgement of our shared knowledge which determines how I will refer to
things. This shared knowledge is an example of social knowledge and in
itself poses problems for development. (In fact, some readers may have
been momentarily confused by my use of *her* to refer to the dog. This is an
example of a pragmatic inference based on cultural assumptions.)

However, the examples I have given of some different features of
language use do not really capture the full extent of our abilities when
using language. For example, Bransford and his colleagues first showed
how people frequently bring their background knowledge to bear on
the comprehension of utterances. One example of this is the study by
Johnson, Bransford and Solomon (1973). They presented adult subjects
with short passages like the following.

The farmer must be warned of the oncoming flood the sheriff cried. He mounted as quickly as possible since he knew that it would take quite a while to spread all the news.

Following presentation of the passages, Johnson *et al.* presented the subjects with recognition sentences like *The sheriff mounted his horse as quickly as possible since he knew that it would take quite a while to spread all the news*. The subjects invariably said that they had heard the sentence before. Thus, they falsely recognized the sentence as the one that they had heard. What this implies is that people implicitly fill in the gaps in what they hear from their background store of knowledge. People automatically assume that the sheriff mounted a horse, even though this was not explicitly stated in the text. Notice that this really is knowledge of the world, in particular knowledge of a specific culture. In another culture, the equivalent of a sheriff might mount a camel or a donkey rather than a horse. Our use of non-linguistic or pragmatic knowledge, therefore, is very pervasive in our everyday discourses.

Similarly, our use of social knowledge is much richer than the perception of shared knowledge that I described above. For example, Schegloff (1968) has shown how skilled we are at turn taking in conversations and has indicated many of the subtle cues that we used in this respect. Similarly, Grice (1975) and more recently Clark (1979) have emphasized the social aspects of cooperation and politeness that are required for successful communication. In particular, they emphasize the ease with which people can interpret the intended meaning of an utterance rather than the literal meaning. Even young children seem quite good at this. When asked *Can you tell me your name?* children usually respond to the intended request for information and say their name. It might be reasonable to assume that they are shy if they respond to the literal question and simply answer *yes*.

These observations suggest that language use is so deeply embedded in other aspects of social and cultural knowledge that it must be impossible to study in isolation. But I think that this is not the case. We can easily find examples to show that the linguistic component can be distinguished from these other sources of knowledge. For example, Slobin (1966) presented adult subjects with a picture of a ball being kicked by a boy and then presented them with the sentence *The ball was kicked by the boy*. He then asked the subjects to say as quickly as possible whether or not the sentence was a true description of the picture. The subjects were very quick at making these decisions. By contrast, when the picture showed a boy being hit by a girl followed by the sentence *The boy was hit by the girl*, the subjects were much slower at making the decision. One reason why the responses were so fast in the first case might be because the sentence can be understood purely by examining the major words. When we see the words *boy*, *kick* and *ball*, it is immediately obvious what action is being described. There is only one possibility. Thus the sentence can be interpreted purely on the basis of the major words and a consideration of possible events in the world.

On the other hand, this is not the case with the second sentence. If we look only at the major words, *boy*, *hit* and *girl* and consider the possible events in the world that could be described by those words, then two events are possible. Either the boy does the hitting or the girl does the hitting. It is only by examining the order of the words (the syntax of the sentence) that the second sentence can be understood.

Thus, there are at least some occasions when linguistic knowledge must be used for comprehension. However, Slobin's results also suggest how it might be possible to understand the first sentence without recourse to syntax. (This interpretation has been queried though, e.g. Forster and Olbrei 1973.) But it does seem likely that young children will do this when they do not understand the structure of a sentence that they hear. For example, Strohner and Nelson (1974) have suggested that young children of about two to three years use a 'probable event' strategy to comprehend difficult sentences. When these children do not understand the sentence, they take the key words and use them to interpret the sentence as describing the most probable event that could occur in the world, given that set of words.

However, it seems most likely that sentence *production* would not be possible without a knowledge of syntax. The order of words is crucial for conveying an intended meaning. For example, the sentence *John loves Mary* does not mean the same thing as *Mary loves John*. Although the words are the same in the two sentences, their order is different and it is the order that determines the meaning.

Another example of how we need to distinguish between linguistic and non-linguistic knowledge is taken from an argument of Slobin's (1979). Imagine a mother, a father and a small child playing with a ball in the garden. The father throws the ball to the mother and the mother turns to the child and says:

Daddy gave me the ball.

If children relied on non-linguistic knowledge, they could interpret the situation in some non-linguistic form, use that interpretation to work out what the mother is saying and then how to say the same thing themselves.

Similarly, if children relied on social knowledge about giving and taking, and about agents and recipients, they could again interpret the situation from a social point of view and use that interpretation to work out what the mother was saying and then how to say it themselves.

Here are some of the difficulties. First of all, there are lots and lots of aspects of the environment that could be comprehended by the child and that could be encoded by the language. So the child has got to work out which features in the environment are, in fact, encoded by a particular sentence. Thus, for the cognitive and social knowledge to be sufficient, it is important that the child has interpreted the context in precisely the form above and not, for example, as *I took the ball from Daddy* or even just, *I've (mummy) got the ball*. So the child has got to make the interpretation that actually corresponds to the sentence. But there are all sorts of other distinctions in the environment that the child may notice. It might have started to rain, for example, so the child may have made an interpretation about the weather. It may be nearly teatime, so the child may be thinking about his/her tea. The child may be more interested in getting the ball him/herself than in the fact that his/her mother has it. The possibilities are endless. So just homing in on the appropriate interpretation that matches the sentence is no trivial matter.

In fact, though, the situation is even more difficult than I have indicated. I have not, for example, even touched on the difficulties of how the child learns the syntax. In other words, even if the child does interpret the relevant situation, and so has a conceptual representation of it, just mapping the words that the mother says on to this representation will not solve the problem of learning the syntax.

In Slobin's example, it is the child who has just received the ball from his or her father and wishes to say:

Daddy gave me the ball.

As Slobin points out, the task looks straightforward. The child simply has to learn that the order of the words is actor–action–recipient–object. In addition, the child must realize that the object is either definite (*the*) or indefinite (*a*). But if we consider the variation between different languages, it soon becomes apparent that there is more to this problem than meets the eye. For example, in German, the determiners encode gender, number and case as well as definiteness. It would also be necessary in German to use a determiner for the agent of the sentence which would indicate that the agent was definite, singular, masculine, and also the subject of the sentence. There are other differences between English and German but, more crucially, there are just as many differences between these two languages and other languages in the world.

What this means is that children must discover which of the large number of seemingly arbitrary facts about the world are actually encoded by the language that they hear. In our English example, it suddenly becomes apparent that a large number of possible distinctions are not required. Why do we only indicate that the object is definite and not the subject? Why indicate definiteness by a word that precedes the noun rather than one which follows it? And, as Slobin observes, why *not* indicate other facts that are also obvious – like the gender of the actor and the recipient, or that the action took place recently, or that balls are round, or that the action was witnessed by the speaker.

This is the major puzzle of language development. How do children learn to use the language that they hear in such a short space of time? The example that I have just given suggests that they cannot rely on cognitive or social knowledge alone. Somewhere along the line a knowledge of language itself will have to be learned. Attempts to solve that puzzle form the basis of this book. In fact, nearly every model of language development assumes that children have sentence–meaning pairs available to aid learning. It seems impossible to see how learning could develop without this assumption. The theories differ in how they assume that the syntax of the language is learned, given these sentence–meaning pairs. The second part of Slobin's argument shows that this is not a simple matter. The first part shows that the assumption that children use sentence–meaning pairs still requires a precise explanation.

This distinction between linguistic and non-linguistic knowledge implies that we cannot consider language use without an understanding of how people use their knowledge of syntax in producing and understanding sentences. In fact, this discussion on the different components of language use is really concerned with linguistic performance. Performance is quite distinct from competence and so it is to that distinction that I now turn.

Competence and performance

Linguistic models of language are competence models. They describe the abstract system of rules that characterizes a person's knowledge of language. It is this knowledge that enables people to have intuitions about the grammaticality of sentences they have never heard before. A competence model, therefore, is designed to account for our ability to decide whether or not a sentence is grammatical. A competence model is not intended to account for the comprehension or production of sentences. For example, you may well be able to say that the following sentence is ungrammatical:

(1) This is the girl who Mary liked Sue.

This decision reflects your linguistic competence. But you are also quite likely to hear a sentence like (1) being said by someone in a conversation. The Watergate tapes (Gold 1974), for example, are full of such speech 'errors'. This is because production is subject to performance factors such as limits on memory, choosing a particular linguistic structure to express an idea, and the need to produce the sentence in a certain left to right sequence. Similarly, comprehension reflects performance factors over and above our knowledge of language. Although we know, for example, that sentence (1) is ungrammatical, in an appropriate context we may still understand what is being said. We have cognitive skills other than language that enable us to decipher the meaning of a message. This distinction between competence and performance – between judgements of grammaticality and comprehension or production – is an important one when we consider the development of language.

Studies of syntactic development aim to account for how children move from their early one-word utterances to full adult knowledge. That is, they aim to explain the course of development from children's performance to adult competence. We should be wary, though, of finding a direct link between these two. Children's performance is manifest in comprehension and production, adult competence is manifest in grammaticality judgements. Thus, the evidence from children is evidence about performance; and that is very different from the evidence used to test a competence model.

In fact, many researchers have tried to circumvent this problem by trying to relate children's competence to adult competence. That is, they have used the children's performance data – comprehension or production – to infer the nature of children's competence. For example, several researchers (e.g. Brown 1973a, Schlesinger 1977) have argued that a child's grammar is based on semantic categories such as agent, experiencer, patient, rather than on syntactic categories such as subject and object. The task has then been to explain how this semantically based grammar develops into a syntactically based one. Other people (e.g. Kuczaj 1982) have suggested that a child's grammar is a simple left to right, 'surface structure' grammar, and the task here has been to explain how this surface structure grammar develops into a more complex grammar, for example a transformational grammar of the kind proposed by Chomsky (1965).

But these are attempts to infer the nature of a child's competence from data derived from performance and should be treated cautiously. It is not yet clear to us how adult performance relates to competence. We have no rules, if you like, for making the necessary inferences from performance to competence. For the moment, let us note that the way children comprehend and produce utterances may tell us more about the social context of those utterances than about the nature of the child's language.

When reviewing the work on syntactic development, we will keep in mind the question of whether we are discussing competence models or performance models. In particular, we need to keep in mind three distinct questions. One is how we can characterize a child's developing linguistic system. The second is how we can characterize the adult's linguistic system and the third is what the relationship is between the child's developing system and the end state of the adult.

Because we need to keep these questions in mind, I will frequently refer throughout the course of this book to work on adults as well as children. However, alongside these questions, we need to keep clear the distinction between competence and performance. More specifically, we need to consider how children move from producing and comprehending utterances of their language to being able to do not only that (as in a performance model) but also have intuitions about whether or not an utterance is grammatical (the product of a competence model).

The goals of a theory of language development

A complete theory of language development needs to consider not only linguistic knowledge – both competence and performance – but also all the different knowledge sources that contribute to language use. Indeed, many studies of language development seem to confuse these distinctions and draw conclusions about linguistic knowledge from data that primarily reflect the use of non-linguistic or pragmatic knowledge. For example, I have already observed that young children can interpret sentences that they do not understand, just by using a 'probable event' strategy. This suggests that young children may use a variety of non-linguistic strategies to 'get by' before a knowledge of the language is fully developed – just as adults do when faced with communicating in a foreign country.

The aim of this book is to attempt to show two things: first, that the major puzzle of language development – the development of syntax – needs to be considered independently of non-linguistic aspects of language use. I hope to show that this tactic has produced some major breakthroughs in our understanding of such development in recent years. The second aim is to consider the ways in which non-linguistic knowledge – both cognitive and social – can contribute to an overall theory of language development.

Suggested readings

The book by Bransford (1979) on human cognition is a good introduction to the nature of adult skills, both linguistic and non-linguistic. Slobin's (1979) chapter on language acquisition in the second edition of his book *Psycholinguistics* is a rich source of ideas and information. To see how people have tried to relate cognitive development to language development, the book by Rice and Kemper (1984) on *Child Language and Cognition* gives a clear and accurate account. Similarly, Bruner's (1983) book on *Child's Talk* does the same from the social point of view. For a linguist's viewpoint on the problem of language acquisition, I recommend Baker's (1979) paper in the journal *Linguistic Inquiry*.

CHAPTER 2

Syntactic Development

We have seen that the meaning of a sentence depends not only on the meanings of the individual words but also on their order. In other words, we need to consider the syntax of sentences. So I will turn now to consider how syntax is acquired by young children.

We can begin by considering the views of Pinker (1979) on what needs to be accounted for in a theory of language development. Pinker has proposed that any plausible theory of language learning will have to account for the fact that all normal children succeed in learning a language; it will have to be consistent with our knowledge of what language is; and it will have to be consistent with the stages the child passes through in learning language. More specifically, Pinker proposes a number of conditions that need to be met by an adequate theory of language learning.

First, we have to account for the *fact* that language can be learned in the first place. This is the *learnability* condition. The ease with which language is learned can be contrasted with the relative difficulty of learning things such as chess, calculus and other complex cognitive skills. Second is the *equipotentiality* condition. A child must be capable of learning any grammar. There would be no point in specifying an innate grammar of English. Third is the *time* condition. Language should be learnable in a normal time period. It is usually assumed that it takes about three years for the basic components of language to be learned. Fourth, the learning mechanism must not require as input types or amounts of information that are unavailable to a child. This is the *input* condition. Fifth, the theory should make predictions about the intermediate stages of acquisition. Children produce successive approximations to the adult grammar during development and do not acquire a full blown adult system immediately. This is the *developmental* condition. Sixth is the *cognitive* condition. The mechanisms described by the theory should not be wildly inconsistent with what is known about the cognitive abilities of children, such as conceptual abilities, memory, attention and so on.

It should not be a surprise to discover that, according to Pinker, no current theory of language learning either satisfies or even addresses all six conditions. Psychologists have tended to concentrate on the input, developmental, cognitive and time conditions. Input has been considered from the point of view of a mother's speech to a child. Much work has been devoted to showing that mothers tend to use a simplified language with their children (Snow 1972), and subsequent work has focused on the possible function of this input (e.g. Barnes, Gutfreund, Satterley and Wells 1983). However, no clear cut function has yet been found for this simplified input during language development (e.g. Richards 1986). Indeed, as Pinker points out, it is possible that a simplified input may make language learning *harder* rather than easier for the child, since it makes it less likely that children will encounter complex sentences of the kind they will eventually acquire.

The developmental condition has been extensively studied and many attempts have been made to characterize the grammar of young children's early word combinations. For example, Braine (1963) suggested that young children used what he termed 'pivot' grammars when they were at the two-word stage. That is, children appear to use a small class of pivot words, such as *more*, *up*, and *allgone*, which can be in either first or second position in the sentence, and a larger class of words, mainly nouns, that tend to have a fixed position in the utterance. More recently, as we shall see, the trend has moved away from trying to characterize children's grammars. Instead, people are trying to see how children's early utterances might form the basis for acquisition of the adult grammar.

Psychologists have considered the cognitive condition by examining the relationship between linguistic and cognitive abilities. This has led a number of people to assume that language develops as a consequence of more general cognitive abilities. Indeed, it makes sense to say that children (usually!) talk only about things they already know about. But there is a stronger claim that children first describe *meanings* and do not use syntax at all. I call this the meaning view and I will discuss this view shortly, when I consider the work of Bowerman (1982) and Anderson's (1976, 1983) computer model of language development that also makes this assumption.

Finally, many psychologists have studied the time course of language development. The now classic studies of Roger Brown (1973a) and his associates are examples of the way children's speech has been patiently transcribed and examined over the course of development. These naturalistic studies have proved a rich source of information about the nature of young children's language. However, they have failed to yield a clear *theoretical* account of language development; rather they have provided rich and detailed descriptions of children's language at different times. In this chapter, we will consider more recent accounts that have attempted to provide a theoretical analysis of the way in which developmental change may come about.

The equipotentiality and the learnability conditions have primarily been the concern of linguists. Thus linguists study the universal features of language (equipotentiality) rather than language-specific properties and attempt to constrain their theories of grammar to those that are learnable in a finite time (learnability). This latter condition has also been extensively studied by computational linguists (e.g. Gold 1967) whose work is only just beginning to have an impact on psychological views of language development. It seems likely that there will need to be more cross-collaboration between psychologists, theoretical linguists and computational linguists if we are to develop a theory of language development that incorporates all of Pinker's conditions.

We will start our survey of psychological models of language development with the notion of transformational grammar and Chomsky's view of language acquisition. I will consider first, the 'traditional' view based on Chomsky's (1965) model of transformational grammar. After that I will discuss two alternative views of syntactic development: one which proposes that children learn syntactic categories on the basis of more concrete semantic categories; and one which proposes that children learn syntactic categories by generalizing from the examples that they hear. Finally, in the next chapter, I will discuss the 'modern' transformational view, which is based on Chomsky's (1981a) theory of government and binding.

Transformational grammar: the standard theory

This view of acquisition sees the child as possessing a 'language acquisition device'. This language acquisition device takes sentences as input and derives from them a grammar. When this notion was incorporated into the psychological literature, the child was viewed as an hypothesis tester. On this hypothesis testing view, the child developed hypotheses about the nature of the grammar and tested them against the input. Psycholinguists assumed that the kind of grammar being acquired was a transformational grammar. In a transformational grammar, there are two major components, an abstract deep structure and a surface structure. The deep structure consists of a syntactic component and a semantic component. The surface structure consists of a syntactic component and a phonological component (see Figure 2.1).

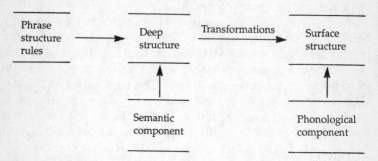

Figure 2.1. A schematic characterization of transformational grammar (Chomsky 1965)

For Chomsky, the critical features of this model are those on the top line of Figure 2.1. The top line contains all the syntactic apparatus of the model: the phrase structure rules which generate the deep structure and transformational rules which convert the deep structure into the surface structure.

I will concentrate here on the syntactic component. One example of the use of syntactic rules is in the derivation of a passive sentence, such as:

Mary was kicked by John.

Deep structures are generated by phrase structure rules of the following kind:

S → NP VP
NP → N
N → *John*
VP → V NP
V → *kick*
NP → DET N
N → *ball*

Phrase structure rules are rewrite rules. They take an element on the left (e.g. S) and rewrite it in smaller units on the right (e.g. NP VP). The end result of the phrase structure rules can be illustrated by means of a tree diagram like the one in Figure 2.2.

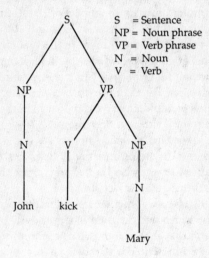

S   = Sentence
NP = Noun phrase
VP = Verb phrase
N = Noun
V = Verb

Figure 2.2

Figure 2.2 shows the deep structure that would be generated by the phrase structure rules. To derive a passive surface structure, the PASSIVE transformation rule had to be applied. This consisted of the following transformations:

1. Transpose the two noun phrases (*John* and *Mary*).
2. Add the preposition *by*.
3. Add the auxiliary *be*.
4. Add inflections to the verbs (i.e. *was kicked*).

This yields the surface structure:

Mary was kicked by John.

A second example is the use of the PRONOMINALIZATION transformation, as in the sentence:

John kicked Mary and *she* ran away.

This sentence was assumed to have an underlying deep structure in which the NP *Mary* is repeated. So it would have a deep structure of the following (simplified) form:

John kicked Mary and *Mary* ran away.

The PRONOMINALIZATION transformation was assumed to look for repeated noun phrases and replace the second occurrence of the noun phrase with a pronoun (of the appropriate number and gender).

The above examples illustrate the model of transformational grammar which was proposed by Chomsky in 1957 and 1965. This was the model adopted as a model of acquisition. In the 1960s this same model of transformational grammar provided a psychological model for adult performance as well as for acquisition. In retrospect it has suffered the same fate in both cases. For example, the demise of transformational grammar in models of adult language can be seen in the work of Sachs (1967) and of Johnson-Laird and Stevenson (1970). Both studies cast doubt on Miller's (1962) view that sentences are stored in deep structure form together with 'transformational footnotes' which specify what transformations have to be applied to convert the stored deep structure back to the original surface structure.

Sachs asked subjects to say whether a given recognition sentence was identical with one which had occurred in a previously presented prose passage. She found that if the target sentence was in the active form, and the subjects were presented with either a passive or an active recognition sentence, then subjects were just as likely to recognize falsely the passive form of the target sentence as they were to recognize correctly the original active form. Miller's hypothesis would predict that if someone hears an active sentence, the passive transformations would not be stored in memory and therefore subjects would be unlikely to say that a passive recognition sentence was the one that was originally heard.

This suggests that a 'strong' view (Fodor 1971) of the psychological reality of transformational grammar is unfounded. However, it could still be argued that a sentence is represented in memory as its linguistic deep structure without assuming a one to one correspondence between linguistic (transformational) operations and psychological operations. In other words, we can hold a 'weak' view of the psychological reality of transformational grammar (Fodor 1971), in that a sentence *is* stored in its deep structure form but this representation is arrived at via certain heuristic devices which operate on the surface structure and do not correspond to the formal transformations relating deep structure to surface structure in the grammar. Sachs's data are compatible with such a view since it can be argued that while the subjects had forgotten which particular transformation (active or passive) had been applied to the test sentence, they did remember its deep structure, since changed meaning sentences were not falsely recognized as target sentences.

However, this 'weak' view seems doubtful in the light of the results of Johnson-Laird and Stevenson (1970). They found that if subjects were not informed of a subsequent memory test, they tended to confuse in their memory the sentence *John liked the painting and bought it from the duchess* with other sentences such as *The painting pleased John and the duchess sold it to him* which have different deep structures but similar meanings. This suggests that in normal discourse, where the listener is not deliberately trying to memorize what is said, the deep structure relations of a sentence are not remembered.

Models of language acquisition based on transformational grammar appear to have suffered the same fate, though at a later time. Just as with adults, the acquisition data was at first supportive of transformational grammar (Brown and Herrnstein (1975) give a good review of this literature), but when stronger tests were made, the model was no longer supported. Some examples of this lack of support follow.

As far as acquisition was concerned, the standard assumption was that the more complex the structure, the later it would be acquired. One example of the failure of transformational grammar is the acquisition of short passives such as

Mary was kicked.

Transformational grammar assumed that a short passive like this was derived from a full passive like the following:

Mary was kicked (by someone).

This means that the short passive should be more complex than the full passive because it requires an extra (DELETION) transformation. Hence the short passive should be acquired later than the full passive. But this is not the case. It appears that short passives are acquired at least as early as long passives, if not earlier. For example, short passives are found in the spontaneous speech of five-year olds but long passives are not (Harwood 1959); children are more likely to use short passives than long passives to describe pictures (Stevenson and Emslie, unpublished data); and comprehension of short passives appears to develop as early as, or earlier than comprehension of the corresponding long ones (Maratsos and Abramovitch 1974).

Another example concerns the use of sentences containing a second subject, such as

John wants Mary to win.

In the above example, the second subject (*Mary*) is explicitly mentioned. But in some sentences the second subject is null, as in the following example:

Peter wants to win.

Again, transformational grammar assumed that such a sentence, containing a null subject, was derived from one which contained the missing subject. Hence the deep structure of the sentence, above, could be described as

Peter wants Peter to win.

A DELETION transformation then deleted the second occurrence of *Peter* to yield the surface structure. This meant that null subject sentences were more complex than sentences that contained an explicit subject, such as, *John wants Mary to win*. They required an extra DELETION transformation.

So null subject sentences should be acquired later than overt subject sentences. Again, however, this does not seem to be the case. Null subject sentences appear earlier than overt subject sentences in both spontaneous speech (Limber 1975) and descriptions of pictures (Stevenson and Emslie, unpublished data).

It was data like the above, along with changing attitudes in both linguistics and psychology, which led to the demise of transformational grammar as a useful principle in acquisition as well as in adult performance. Since that demise, there have been many different proposals for the acquisition of syntax. I will just give a brief account of three of the more influential ones.

1. Children use their prior acquisition of meaning as a basis for the learning of syntax (e.g. Anderson 1976, 1983, Bowerman 1982, Braine and Hardy 1982 and Schlesinger 1977).
2. Children make syntactic generalizations from the sentences that they hear (e.g. Maratsos 1982, Maratsos and Chalkley 1980).
3. Children come equipped with a universal grammar. On exposure to

the linguistic input, a number of open parameters in the innate universal grammar become fixed in specific ways. This is the 'parameter setting' view. (It is so called to distinguish it from the earlier 'hypothesis testing' view of traditional transformational grammar.) This parameter setting view is the modern linguistic view, based on Chomsky's (1981a, b) government binding theory.

In this chapter, I will discuss the first two proposals. I will devote Chapter 3 to the third proposal. So let us consider first the view that children acquire syntax on the basis of their knowledge of meaning. There are several different versions of this 'meaning view'. I will concentrate first on the position of Bowerman (1982).

The meaning view

According to this view, when children first start to speak, they are not using the syntactic categories of noun, verb, adjective etc. or of subject, object. Instead they are expressing semantic notions such as agent, action and patient or recipient. In other words, the child has already categorized the world into notions such as actions and things; and things have already been further categorized into actors, patients and recipients. So children start producing sentences in terms of these conceptual or semantic relations and not in terms of syntactic relations. These semantic relations are less abstract than syntactic relations and are more obvious in the environment. Thus, children describe agents acting on patients; they are not producing subject verb object sequences.

The main evidence to support this view comes from the things children say at the early stages of language use. These utterances seem to express semantic relationships rather than syntactic ones. For example, the earliest verbs that children use are usually action verbs. Hence two word utterances express agent–action relations or action–object relations. Young children seem less likely to use verbs that do not express actions. Thus they are more likely to say

Hit ball.

which expresses an action, rather than

See ball.

which is a state, or something that happens.

It is also argued that the notions of agent, action and patient represent the 'canonical' sentence form at this stage. That is, children regard agent action patient sequences as the prototypical or normal form for sentences. And it is through the use of these semantic categories that the child first expresses syntactic categories, such as noun and verb, and subject–object.

The main question, then, for this view, is how the child is able to change from a semantic based grammar to a syntactic based grammar; that is, a grammar which is based on syntactic categories such as noun, verb and adjective, and on more abstract syntactic categories such as subject, verb and object – regardless of *semantic* role. This is not an easy question, because the relationship between syntax and semantics is not a direct one.

Take, for example, the notion of subject. The subject of a sentence does not express a single semantic notion – the notion of agent, for example. Instead, the subject of a sentence can express a variety of semantic roles and hence cuts across the early categories that the child knows. The sentences below show how the subject of a sentence can express such a variety of semantic roles:

John opened the door.	Subject is an agent.
The door opened.	Subject is a recipient.
The key opened the door.	Subject is an instrument.
John saw the door.	Subject is an experiencer.
Manchester is rainy.	Subject is a location.

These examples show that the relationship between semantics and syntax is not a direct one. So how does the child get from a semantic system to a syntactic system?

Bowerman (1982) proposes that there is a reorganization of the grammar. There is a change from a semantic to a syntactic system. Bowerman gives many examples to support this notion of a reorganization from semantics to syntax. One example concerns the prefix *un*, as in *uncover*. Bowerman points out that the meaning of the prefix is to convey the opposite meaning to that of the verb. In English, the prefix is restricted to a certain class of verbs: in general, those that encode particular actions, namely, to *cover*, *enclose* and *attach to a surface*.

Now, this particular restriction has nothing to do with cognitive categories. There is nothing in the cognitive system that would make these verbs into a special category where actions can be undone. For example, we can undo the action of adding two numbers but we do not have a verb *to unadd*. Instead, we have the verb *to subtract*. So the prefix specifies a specific linguistic category that is not one of the child's semantic categories. Bowerman's data indicate that when her children first used the prefix, it was used appropriately. It was initially used only in words that the children had already heard.

Thus words like *uncover* and *unfasten* were used appropriately. But shortly after this, the prefix was generalized to new words. It was applied to any verb to reverse its action e.g. *unstraighten*. Thus the children seemed to have generalized the prefix on the basis of a general cognitive principle (reversing an action), but not on a specific linguistic principle. Later, the prefix was restricted to the appropriate class of verbs. In particular, errors that were still made were applied to verbs that themselves reverse the action of covering, enclosing or attaching to a surface. For example, at one point Bowerman's daughter Eve said

Will you unopen them.

This, then, is evidence for the initial piecemeal acquisition of a semantically based language (hence overextensions based on meaning). This subsequently changes into a linguistic or syntactic system by a process of reorganization (hence overextensions on the basis of the linguistic category). Bowerman cites many other examples to support this notion of a reorganization from semantics to syntax. It represents a discontinuous view of development: at some point in development the system changes in a very radical way.

The major difficulty with this approach is that it is really a description, not an explanation. There is no explanation of what brings about the change from a semantic to a syntactic system. So if we take this position, we still need an account of how syntax is acquired. In Chapter 1 I used the arguments from Slobin (1979) to show that a transition from a semantic or cognitive system to a syntactic system is not a simple matter. I have also indicated that the grammatical notion of *subject* can be used for a variety of semantic roles. So if we adopt Bowerman's position, we still need an account of how syntax is acquired.

One attempt to develop an account of how children pass from a semantic stage to a syntactic stage of language use comes from Anderson (1976, 1983). Anderson has produced computer simulations which attempt to show how language can be learned on the basis of general cognitive principles rather than specific linguistic rules. On the basis of these simulations, Anderson suggests that children can learn the syntax of a language purely on the basis of non-linguistic knowledge.

Anderson (1976) suggests that children have access to a series of pairs consisting of a sentence and its meaning, which can be inferred from the non-linguistic context. The child's task during learning is to identify a function which maps sentences on to meanings. The sentences are represented in a surface syntactic form, while the meaning of the sentence is the cognitive representation of the non-linguistic event and this is in the form of semantic networks.

The cognitive representation is very similar to the representation devised by Anderson and Bower (1973) in their semantic memory model called human associative memory. This consists of concepts defined by nodes in the network together with links from that node to other, related nodes.

Given that children have these two forms of representation available they make use of both of them in learning the language. Thus, children try to match concepts in the meaning structure to words in the sentence. At the same time, they try to fit a tree structure for meaning (the semantic nets) on to a tree structure for the sentence. They do this by trying to rearrange the structure of the semantic net. For example, imagine a situation where a boy kisses a girl. A child will interpret this situation and deduce that it consists of the following semantic propositions:

1. X is a boy.
2. X is small.
3. Y is a girl.
4. X kisses Y.

This can be represented in a meaning representation like the one shown in Figure 2.3. In Figure 2.3 P1 stands for the complete proposition, the letter X represents an instance of a boy and the letter Y an instance of a girl.

If the child then hears the sentence *The boy kisses the girl*, the

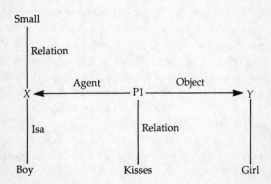

Figure 2.3

conceptual structure, or meaning representation, can be rearranged so that it fits the words in the sentence to yield a conceptual structure like the one in Figure 2.4.

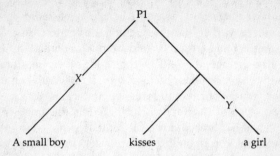

Figure 2.4

Just as in Figure 2.3, in this figure, P1 stands for the complete proposition, the letter *X* stands for a boy and the letter *Y* stands for a girl.

Thus the child hypothesizes two main constituents: the first is something that is both small and a boy. The second is the action of kissing a girl. So in the above example, the child can hypothesize that the first major constituent of a sentence refers to an individual that is the subject of an underlying proposition.

One problem with this approach is that there are many ways to fit a semantic structure on to a string of words, only one of which will correspond to the correct breakdown of the sentence into its syntactic constituents. For example, nothing prevented the child with coming up with the following conceptual structure to fit the situation shown in Figure 2.5.

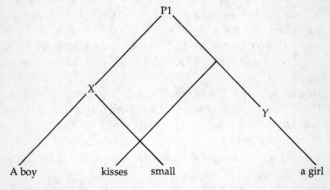

Figure 2.5

Anderson proposes two mechanisms to ensure that the child selects the right conceptual structure. First, the child must already know what the main proposition of a sentence is and what is being asserted. This, Anderson claims, is gleaned from pragmatic information from adults during normal interaction. Second, there is a constraint on network formation that says that branches are not allowed to cross each other. This constraint would stop the child from considering an ill formed structure like the one above. This constraint on crossing branches is known as the *graph deformation condition*. It essentially constrains the form of the grammar that a child will hypothesize.

The next stage of development comes after this initial period in which the child has broken down the sentences into constituents and hypothesized the corresponding rewrite rules. In this next stage, the child needs to be able to *combine* rules derived from different sentences. If this were not possible, the child would end up with one rule for each sentence, which would place impossible memory constraints on the child.

Hence, this next phase makes use of *rule merging*. Children will merge rules on the basis of meaning, i.e. on the similarity of semantic representations. Anderson proposes that words in the same positions in different sentences which have identical semantic roles can be merged into one class. For example, imagine that after the above situation, the child encounters the sentence *A tall man greets a woman*, along with its associated semantic structure. The semantic structure will be identical to that for *A small boy kisses a girl* and semantic similarity will ensure that *kisses* is equated with *greets*, *small* is equated with *tall*, *boy* is equated with *man* and so on. This structural and semantic similarity allows the child to merge the equivalent words into one class and then to merge the higher level constituents into one class (equivalent to a subject noun phrase, for example). The merging of words into classes and constituents into classes would allow the child to produce 16 different sentences after having heard just the two above. Thus the child might produce *A tall boy greets a girl*, *A small man kisses a woman* and so on.

Anderson calls this the semantics induced equivalence of syntax, and claims that there is a tendency in natural language always to use the same syntactic construction to express a particular semantic relationship. Overall, this model represents an implementation of the semantic view of language learning and removes the need for innate language-specific structures.

However, there are a number of difficulties associated with this model. Pinker (1979) lists a number of them. First, we have already seen that there is no one to one relationship between syntax and semantics, so the semantics induced equivalence of syntax will not account for the development of syntax that does not correspond with semantics. An additional example of this problem is that rule merging on the basis of semantic similarity would lead to the production of sentences which do not appear in the language. For example, we can consider the following three sentences where the verbs are semantically similar.

John gave the book to Bill.
John transferred the money to Geneva.
John donated the painting to the museum.

If rules were merged on the basis of this similarity, then on hearing

John gave Bill the book.

the child would hypothesize the existence of the equivalent sentences:

John transferred Geneva the money.
John donated the museum the painting.

A second problem is how the child arrives at the relevant semantic representation of the situation. We considered this problem in Chapter 1 and regarded it as a major puzzle for language development. Anderson sidesteps the problem in his model by stipulating that the child already knows what is being asserted in a situation. However, it is also worth noting that even if this were not a problem, and children were able to map non-linguistic interpretations of situations on to sentences, this still would not resolve Slobin's additional problems raised in Chapter 1 concerning *which* aspects of a situation are actually encoded by the language being learned. In addition, as Pinker points out, one reason that Anderson's model works as well as it does is because the semantic representation is almost identical to the syntactic representation. The model does not allow for the possibility that meaning and syntax are different in structure.

Taken together, these comments on Anderson's model indicate that it fails the learnability condition. A child could not learn a language in the way proposed by Anderson. The model also fails the equipotentiality condition. The graph deformation condition rules out crossing branches in both the semantic and the syntactic representations. However, while this constraint applies to most sentences in a language like English where syntax is primarily coded through word order, it does not apply to inflected languages like Russian, which frequently have elements of one phrase interrupted by those from another. In his later simulation (1983) Anderson proposes that when sentences violate this graph deformation condition, it is necessary to learn the transformations underlying these sentences. However, Anderson's model can learn these tranformations only with great difficulty.

Nevertheless, Anderson's model is an impressive attempt to implement the semantic view of language acquisition. The difficulty of the task, though, may be evidenced by Anderson's weakening of his claims that language can be learned in the same way as any other cognitive skill. In his 1985 book Anderson comments that the issue of whether or not there are language-specific mechanisms is still an open one which can be determined only by detailed empirical and theoretical efforts. So we are still faced with the problem of how children learn syntax if they do not do it by means of semantic generalizations.

Perhaps we should turn, therefore, to our second proposal concerning the acquisition of syntax.

Inductive generalizations

Maratsos and Chalkley (1980) propose that children learn syntax by inductive generalizations. Specifically, in contrast to the meaning view, Maratsos and Chalkley argue that syntactic categories such as noun, verb and adjective are so different from semantic categories that they cannot be learned purely on the basis of semantics. Verbs are not just 'doing' words, for example.

Hence they propose that children learn which words belong in a particular syntactic category (verbs, say) by noticing a set of correlated features which, in general, co-occur whenever that category is used.

More specifically, like Bowerman, Maratsos and Chalkley agree that children's initial utterances describe agent–action–recipient sequences. However, in contrast to Bowerman, they argue that these sequences are not a reflection of semantic categories. The children are simply using words to describe their concepts directly. Thus, Bowerman proposes that children have formed semantic categories such as agents, objects and actions; and it is these categories that underlie children's early utterances. But for Maratsos and Chalkley, when a child says something like *Daddy hit ball*, he or she is not using *Daddy* as an instance of the class of agents, or *hit* as an instance of the class of actions. Instead, he or she is saying that that particular person is hitting that particular thing, exactly as he or she perceives it. Subsequently, at about three years, children are able to analyse a word into its parts (e.g. a verb and its ending). When they can do this, they then form syntactic categories so that verbs, for example, are the words that have particular endings such as *-ed*. Hence the children are no longer describing actions, they are using the syntactic category of a verb.

Maratsos (1982) illustrates this use of correlated features by a comparison of the very *like* with the adjective *fond*. As he points out, if children form generalizations on the basis of meaning, then they should treat these two words as if they were the same. Being fond of someone is very similar in meaning to liking someone. Certainly they are more similar in meaning than the two verbs *like* and *kill*.

However, Maratsos goes on to propose that children distinguish between *like* and *fond* because they are associated with different sets of syntactic features. In the present tense, the verb *like* takes the suffix *-s* or nothing at all. On the other hand, use of the adjective, *fond*, in the present tense is preceded by the verb *to be*. Thus we have

She like*s* it.   She *is* fond of it.

I like it.   I *am* fond of it.

From these correlated features, the child is then able to predict the forms of the past tenses:

She like*d* it.   She *was* fond of it.

Thus, the child notices these sets of correlated features (the endings for verbs; the use of *to be* for adjectives) and uses these to categorize the words into syntactic classes.

There are two arguments to support this position. One argument is that when children use the past tense of verbs like *saw*, or *heard*, they overgeneralize the syntactic rule and produce *seed* or *hearded* instead. The child notices the features of the present tense:

I see.
She sees.

From these present tense endings, the child predicts that the past tense will contain the suffix *-ed* (hence *seed*). The earlier, correct, forms of these verbs occur before the child has formed the relevant syntactic generalizations.

A second argument is based on the *failure* to observe certain kinds of errors. For example, children do not treat adjectives as if they were verbs. Children do not say *She fonded it*; they do not make the kinds of errors you would expect if children were forming the category of verb on the basis of meaning. Thus *like* and *kill* are in the same category, but *fond* is not. However, Bowerman has observed these kinds of errors, so this evidence is not clear cut.

But the problem with this position has been pointed out by Gleitman and Wanner (1982). Maratsos and Chalkley say that a child learns the verb category, for example, by learning that it usually has -*ed* as the past tense inflection. But this presupposes that the child already knows that verbs have a syntactic means for marking tense. Thus, the child must recognize that the -*ed* is a tense marker. This recognition is necessary because other words, particularly adjectives, also end in -*ed* – *lighthearted*, for example. Similarly, recognizing -*s* as the present tense inflection presupposes that the child can recognize the present tense inflection and distinguish it from the plural -*s* on nouns.

So, the Maratsos model still leaves a lot of grammatical knowledge unexplained; for example, knowledge that -*s* on the end of a word means one thing if the word is a verb and another if the word is a noun. Hence the child needs to know the category in order to recognize the inflection. This still leaves us, then, with the original puzzle. How might the child form syntactic categories? Like Bowerman's approach, this theory offers no real solution to the question.

Suggested readings

The standard theory of transformational grammar had a more long lasting influence on studies of language development than on studies of adult performance. Brown's (1973b) article in the *American Psychologist* is a good example of this tradition. Dale's (1976) book on *Language Development* gives a more detailed account of this approach. Explicit refutations of the view that children acquire a transformational grammar are hard to find. Perhaps the best source is Section IV of Maratsos's (1979) chapter, 'How to get from words to sentences' in Aaronson and Reiber (eds) *Perspectives in Psycholinguistics*. The best single source for current views on the learning of syntax is the book by Wanner and Gleitman (1982), *Language Acquisition: The State of the Art*. Both Bowerman and Maratsos present their views here. In addition, the book's introduction by the editors is a splendid review of current issues in the study of language development.

CHAPTER 3

Language Learning as Parameter Setting

Government binding theory

According to government binding theory, the child learns syntactic categories like nouns and verbs not just on the basis of the input, as the other views assume, but also on the basis of a specific biological endowment concerning the structure of grammar. The basic rationale for this approach is the learnability condition. We can constrain the form of the grammar which children can acquire until the task becomes trivially easy. In Anderson's (1976, 1983) model, we saw an attempt to do this with his graph deformation condition.

This view also takes seriously the equipotentiality condition. The basic grammar is universal: what the child has to learn are the specific rules of the particular language community. So, for example, the child is already equipped with the implicit knowledge that language can be analysed only in particular ways. Thus, one proposal is that the child already knows that a sentence may be analysed according to phrase structure rules.

These phrase structure rules yield tree structures like the one in Figure 3.1 for the sentence:

The small girl lifted the rock.

Given this analysis, the child can then work out which words in the

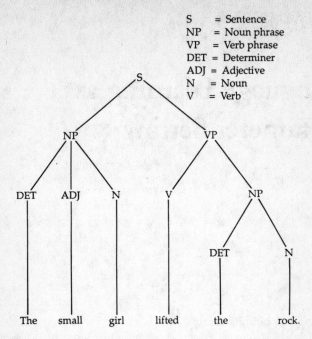

Figure 3.1

language are nouns and which are verbs on the basis of their structural position in the sentence. Thus, nouns and noun phrases occur only in certain positions in this structure. It is words in those positions which take plural inflections. Similarly, verbs always appear after a noun phrase, so it is words in *that* position that take tense inflections. So that is how children can distinguish between the -*s* on the end of a verb and the -*s* on the end of a noun. (If you remember, that is what caused trouble for Maratsos and Chalkley's theory.)

Chomsky's general aim has always been to outline a system of rules that will generate all and only all the grammatical sentences of a language. In standard transformational grammar (1965), the main mechanism for achieving this aim was transformations, such as PASSIVE or PRONOMINALIZATION. In government binding theory (1981a, b), the transformational component has been drastically reduced. The major emphasis now is on specifying constraints on permissible grammatical structures. I will not go into the details of the theory here, but a fuller account can be found in Chapter 7. In this chapter, I will just describe the treatment of pronouns to illustrate how some of the constraints in government binding theory work.

In the standard theory, the grammar specified the antecedent of a pronoun. This is because the antecedent was the earlier mention of the noun phrase that was replaced by the PRONOMINALIZATION transformation. (See Chapter 2 for details of this transformation.) In government binding theory, the PRONOMINALIZATION transformation has been discarded. One reason for this is that, in certain circumstances, the transformation does not yield the preferred interpretation. Take, for example, the sentence

Everyone hoped that he would win.

According to the standard theory, this sentence is derived from an underlying structure similar to

Everyone hoped that everyone would win.

The PRONOMINALIZATION transformation replaces the second *everyone* with the pronoun *he*. Thus the antecedent of the pronoun is the first *everyone*. But this, of course, is not what the sentence means. It does not mean 'everyone hoped that everyone would win'. So the antecedent of the pronoun cannot be *everyone*. In fact, the interpretation of the pronoun is ambiguous. One possible antecedent is *each person*. If everyone consisted of Bill, Joe and Fred, then Bill hoped that Bill would win, Joe hoped that Joe would win, and Fred hoped that Fred would win. Alternatively, Bill, Joe and Fred might have a friend called Simon running in a race. Thus the sentence might mean that Bill, Joe and Fred all hoped that Simon would win. In this case the antecedent of the pronoun is *Simon*. This is the second interpretation of the pronoun.

In either case, the PRONOMINALIZATION transformation gives the wrong antecedent. And the 1965 version of transformational grammar had no principled way of saying *why* the transformation would not work. Hence, the transformation was discarded and, instead, in the current theory of government and binding it is assumed that pronouns are present in the deep structure (now called d-structure) and are not generated by a transformation. However, if a pronoun is already present in the d-structure, then there is no rule for specifying the antecedent. This is where the notion of constraints comes in. The constraints specify which antecedent–pronoun relations are permissible and which are not. Consider, for example, the antecedent of *him* in the following sentence.

John said that Bill liked *him*.

In *principle*, if there were no grammar, either *John* or *Bill* could be antecedents of *him*. (A third person could also be the antecedent but I will ignore that possibility here.) However, government binding theory specifies a constraint on the permissible antecedent–pronoun relations. This constraint is that the antecedent cannot be in the same 'local domain' as the pronoun. The term 'local domain' refers (very loosely) to a clause.

Given this constraint, there is only one grammatical interpretation of the sentence – the one where *John* is the antecedent of *him*. That, then, is a constraint on pronominal interpretation.

In fact, if we did want the sentence to mean 'John said that Bill liked Bill', then a reflexive pronoun would have been used. The constraint on the interpretation of reflexives is the mirror image of the constraint on pronominal interpretation. A reflexive pronoun *must* have an antecedent in its local domain (the same clause). So if we put in a reflexive pronoun, that must refer to *Bill*; it cannot refer to *John*.

John said that Bill liked himself.

There is one additional feature of the constraints on reflexive and pronominal interpretations. The constraints refer to antecedents that are higher in the phrase structure tree than the reflexive or pronoun. Higher in the tree means (roughly) closer to the S node. A simplified phrase structure tree is given in Figure 3.2 for the sentence below.

John said (that) Bill liked him.

The constraint on reflexive interpretation is that it must have an antecedent that is higher in the tree in the same local domain. In Figure 3.2 *Bill* is higher in the tree than *himself*. So *Bill* is the antecedent of *himself*. The constraint on pronominal interpretation is that it *cannot* have an antecedent that is higher in the tree in the same local domain. So *Bill* cannot be the antecedent of *him* in Figure 3.2. Although *John* is also higher in the tree than *him*, it can still be the antecedent because it is not in the same local domain as the pronoun.

So both *John* and *Bill* are higher in the tree than *him* and *himself*. They are both closer to S nodes, than *him* or *himself*. A more technical version of the term 'higher in the tree' is the notion 'c-command' (Reinhart 1983), which says that node A (e.g. *Bill*) c-commands node B (e.g. *him* or *himself*) if node A is higher in the tree than node B. More simply, to decide whether a particular node c-commands another, go to the top of the branch and look at what is underneath it. The technical definition is: node A c-commands node B if the first branching node above node A is higher than node B. Thus *John* c-commands *Bill* in the sentence above, but *Bill* does not c-command *John*.

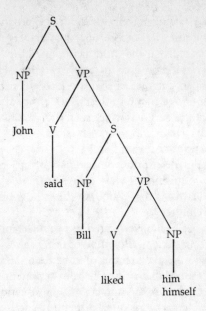

Figure 3.2

The major features that have been introduced here are the notion of a local domain (roughly, the clause) and the structural notion of c-command. Chomsky argues that these notions are crucial for determining whether or not a noun phrase is a permissible antecedent for a pronoun or a reflexive.

In fact, it turns out, that these notions of a local domain and of c-command place constraints on the interpretation of other kinds of sentences too, not just those containing pronouns. According to Chomsky, therefore, these notions form a part of universal grammar. Universal grammar describes the innate principles of grammar. And this brings us to Chomsky's proposals for language acquisition.

Universal grammar consists of a small set of principles (like the notion of local domain and of c-command). But these principles are not completely specified. And the way these principles are used to produce actual sentences varies from one language to another. According to Chomsky, these principles contain open parameters. A parameter is a variable that has to be filled in by experience with the environment. So, for example, the child knows about such structural relations as c-command and local domain. But what the child *does not* know are the precise rules of pronominal and reflexive interpretation that apply in his/her specific language community. It is exposure to a particular language that specifies how those open parameters are fixed. Once these parameters are fixed, the child has attained the 'core grammar'. Hence acquisition is a process of 'parameter setting'. (This notion of a grammar with open parameters that are fixed by experience can be likened to the notion of frames (Minsky 1977), where a 'room frame', for example, contains empty slots for such things as number and types of windows, doors, chairs and so on. The slots are filled by subsequent information in a text or conversation.)

That was a brief description of one part of government binding theory and how acquisition is viewed in that framework. The crucial question is how useful is that framework for understanding language development in children.

This question has been investigated in two different ways. One way is the traditional psychological method of using the theory to generate experimental hypotheses which can then be tested in young children. The general procedure that is used here is to present children with a series of sentences and ask them to act out the situations described by the sentences, using toys. It is often difficult to interpret these experiments because the sentences sometimes have to be very complicated in order to test the theory.

However, one general finding is that, when learning a language, children *do* indicate that they have a knowledge of notions like c-command and local domain. This conclusion emerges from the studies of both Solan (1983) and Deutsch, Koster and Koster (1986). For example, both studies find that reflexive pronouns are understood before non-reflexives. When acting out the situation described by a sentence containing a reflexive, children always choose an antecedent that c-commands the reflexive and that is in the same local domain.

Children have more difficulty in understanding non-reflexive pronouns and the interpretation of this observation is less clear cut. Solan (1983) suggests that the problem for the children is that they treat both types of pronoun in the same way. So they assume that both have a c-commanding antecedent in the same local domain. There is certainly some evidence that when children misunderstand non-reflexives, it is because they have interpreted them in the same way as reflexives (Stevenson and Pickering 1987). So one suggestion is that children assume that interpretations are confined to the same local domain. However, an alternative interpretation has been proposed by Deutsch *et al.* (1986). They suggest that children find pronouns more difficult than reflexives because, unlike reflexives, pronouns cannot be interpreted purely by means of syntax. Thus, for pronouns, children have to bring together their knowledge of syntax with their developing cognitive skills. Again, there is evidence to suggest that the difficulty children have with pronouns is caused largely by the failure to make use of pragmatic cues, not by a failure to use syntactic knowledge (Stevenson and Pickering 1987).

That was an example of the psychological approach to investigating the thesis of government binding theory. Within that approach, people are primarily trying to spell out some of the conditions proposed by Pinker, namely the time, developmental and (in some cases) the cognitive conditions. Investigators are trying to give an explanation for the time span of development by means of specifying the nature of the developmental changes, both linguistic and non-linguistic.

The second way in which linguistic models have been tested is by trying to implement them on a computer. For example, Berwick and Weinberg (1984) take a model of an adult parser and attempt to provide a formal model of acquisition. This is a very ambitious attempt which primarily aims to fulfil the learnability condition. However, Berwick and Weinberg go further and claim that their model can deal with all of the conditions proposed by Pinker. We will see how close they come to confirming that claim.

Berwick and Weinberg's model has three components: an adult model of grammar, the initial state of the child and the syntactic knowledge that is acquired during development. The adult model is based on a computer model of comprehension which uses the principles of government binding theory (Marcus 1980). This 'Marcus parser' contains the core grammar: the basic principles of universal grammar that apply to English, including such notions as local domain and c-command.

The initial state of the child consists of a knowledge of words and their morphology (e.g. that *cats* is the plural of *cat*); a knowledge of the proper assignment of arguments to verbs (e.g. the knowledge that in a sentence like *John kissed Mary*, the verb has two arguments, *John* in the subject position and *Mary* in the object position); and also the basic principles of universal grammar (e.g. the principle of c-command).

The third component is concerned with what syntactic knowledge is acquired and how it is acquired. The child starts with universal grammar and learns the core grammar (i.e. universal grammar with all the parameters fixed as a result of experience). The basic learning principle is that rules are added to the data base one at a time.

So how does the model work? First, the system receives a sentence as input. If the system can parse the sentence with the rules it already has, then there is no change. If, however, the system *cannot* parse the sentence, then it tries to make the smallest possible change to its current rules. If this minimal change now allows the sentence to be parsed, the system adds that change to the data base as a new rule. If the system *cannot* parse the sentence with a single rule change, then the sentence is ignored.

Pinker's conditions for language learning are met in the following ways. The model meets the input condition by accepting only simple sentences (see, e.g., Snow 1972). It meets the time condition because the system learns gradually over time. It meets the cognitive condition because certain rules are acquired as a *consequence* of memory constraints. It meets the developmental condition because it makes the same mistakes as children, but, in addition, spells out why the errors are made. It meets the learnability condition because the grammar to be learned (government binding theory) is so strongly constrained that the learning task becomes relatively trivial. Finally, it addresses the equipotentiality condition because the initial state of the child consists of universal grammar. And it is a fundamental assumption that universal grammar is the prerequisite for learning any language.

The best way to understand the model is to take an example sentence and show how the system parses it. We will begin by showing how Marcus's system parses a simple sentence. Take a sentence like the following:

The boy kisses Mary.

The system builds up a lefthand context, which consists of a memory stack of syntactic categories as the sentence is parsed. The bottom element in the stack is the active node and this consists of the syntactic category currently being tried out on the input. It also has a righthand context, which consists of the next two or three words in the sentence. This is the input buffer.

On initially encountering the above sentence, the currently active node is the sentence, and this is the only element in the lefthand context so far. The input buffer consists of the first three words of the sentence:

The boy kisses

The first word encountered is the determiner *the*. The system knows about phrase structure rules, so it knows that a noun phrase can be rewritten as a determiner plus a noun. Hence it hypothesizes that the first syntactic category in the sentence is a noun phrase. So the new currently active node is now a noun phrase, and the input buffer now contains the words:

boy kisses Mary.

The system has a rule which says if you are looking for a noun phrase attach a noun. This rule 'instructs' the system to look at the first word in the input buffer. If it is a noun, then it is attached to the noun phrase which is then complete. This leaves

kisses Mary.

in the input buffer. Since the next word is a verb, the system will start to look for a verb phrase which consists of a verb plus a noun phrase. The currently active node is now the verb phrase and the associated rule is to look for a noun phrase in the input buffer and attach it to the verb phrase. The only word left in the input buffer is a noun (Mary), so this can be parsed as a noun phrase and attached to the verb phrase. The lefthand context now consists of the following memory stack:

S
NP
VP

This is then interpreted according to the phrase structure rules as a sentence consisting of a noun phrase plus a verb phrase. Hence the sentence is parsed. This is a simple example of how Marcus's parser works.

Now let us take an example of how Berwick and Weinberg's acquisition model might learn additional rules. We will take as our example, the rule of subject-auxiliary verb inversion in questions such as

Will John kiss Mary?

Here, the auxiliary verb *will* and the subject *John* have been switched round to form the question. The system can already parse sentences containing auxiliaries like

John will kiss Mary.

and it cannot learn the inversion rule until it has already learned about auxiliaries.

So, the system is presented with a sentence like the one above (*Will John kiss Mary?*). The first syntactic category in the active node of the lefthand context is the sentence. This instructs the system to look for a noun phrase. However, the first word in the input buffer is the auxiliary *will*, which cannot be parsed as part of a noun phrase. So the system gets stuck. One minimal change that the system will try on getting stuck is to switch round the words in the first two buffer cells. This converts the original input buffer from

Will John kiss

to

John will kiss

With this minimal change, the sentence can now be parsed in a manner analogous to the example taken from Marcus's model. Given that the sentence can now be parsed, the system saves the new switch rule together with the original input buffer pattern. Saving the original input pattern gives the context for applying the rule again. After more examples, this saving of the original input pattern is discarded and a generalization is made by rule merging. Now the rule applies whenever the input buffer contains:

(Auxiliary verb) (noun phrase) (e.g. *Will John*)

This was a simple example. I will very briefly describe how the system learns passive sentences.

First, we need to know a little more detail about government binding theory. This theory has two levels of structure a d-structure (similar to the deep structure) and an s-structure (similar to a surface structure). The two are related by movement rules. Under certain well specified conditions, a noun phrase in a d-structure can be moved to an empty category in d-structure. This changes the word order at s-structure, but leaves a trace in the position that originally contained the noun phrase. Thus, a short passive such as

Mary was kissed.

has the following d-structure

e was kissed Mary.

where *e* stands for an empty noun phrase category.

One general principle of government binding theory is case theory. Case theory claims that every lexically filled (i.e. non-empty) noun phrase must have a case assigned to it either by a verb, by a preposition, or by the feature INFL (INFL, or inflection, refers to verb tense and assigns case to subject nouns). The d-structure above contains the verb *was kissed*. This means that *Mary* cannot be the object of that verb (you cannot *was kiss* someone), so *Mary* has no case assigned to it. By virtue of case theory, this makes it an impermissible d-structure: the lexically full noun phrase (*Mary*) must have case, but does not. However, the empty category (*e*) does have a case assigned to it from the tense of the verb (i.e. from the feature INFL). Hence, the constraints of case theory force the movement of the lexically full noun phrase from a caseless position in the sentence to a cased position. This results in the following s-structure:

Mary(i) was kissed t(i).

The trace *t* stands for the trace of the moved noun phrase and the bracketed letters *i* indicate that *t* and *Mary* are related. (Noun phrase traces have the same properties as reflexive pronouns, so we can say that, in this s-structure, *Mary* is the antecedent of *t*. *Mary* c-commands *t* and is in the same local domain.)

So how does Berwick and Weinberg's system learn to parse short passives? First, as part of the initial state, one of the phrase structure rules that the system knows is that a sentence can be rewritten in the following way:

S → NP INFL VP

INFL indicates tense. In passive sentences like

Mary(i) was kissed t(i).

was is parsed as INFL.

When Berwick and Weinberg's system is presented with short passives like the one above, the first two words will be categorized as NP (*Mary*) and INFL *was*. At this point in the sentence, then, the lefthand stack consists of the following categories:

S
NP
INFL

The remaining items in the input buffer are *kissed t(i)*. The next item (*kissed*) is now removed from the input buffer for analysis by the currently active stack. Since the word is a verb, the system tries to find a noun phrase to attach to the verb to form a verb phrase. However, there is no noun phrase, only a trace. So the attach rule fails and the system cannot parse the sentence. The system now tries one of its minimal changes in an attempt to parse the sentence. For example, the first thing it will try is to switch round the first and second words in the input buffer. Since there are no words in the input buffer, this change is not possible.

The system then tries another minimal change; this time it tries to apply a rule called 'drop trace'. This rule says that if there is a trace in the first buffer cell, remove it. Since there is a trace, this rule can be applied and the trace removed. This means that there is nothing left to analyse in the input buffer. So the system can look elsewhere for a noun phrase to attach to the verb. The obvious place to look is in the memory stack, which contains a noun phrase. Thus, this noun phrase can be attached to the verb to form a verb phrase, resulting in a grammatical parse of the sentence.

The rule 'drop trace' is now stored together with the original input buffer pattern which produces a new rule for passives in that environment. After rule merging, the rule will apply directly to verb–trace environments. This system of learning means that short passives will be learned before full passives like

Mary was kissed by John.

This is compatible with the experimental findings. Indeed it was findings such as these that caused problems for the view that children acquire a transformational grammar. Berwick and Weinberg's model will also initially interpret full passives as if they were actives, which is precisely what young children seem to do (Bever 1970).

Thus, the model seems to account well for some of the facts of language acquisition by making use of an adult grammar based on government binding theory. However, the model is not simply an implementation of government binding theory. Instead, it *simulates* the grammar by means other than the rules of the grammar. It produces this simulation by building in constraints which contribute to its learnability. The model makes use of two kinds of constraint. One kind is specific to the parser. The other is a general principle of language learning.

The specific constraints are constraints on memory. For example, the learner has access to only two nodes in the memory stack and to, at most, three input buffer cells. So the system is highly constrained in terms of memory. It is because of the constraint upon access to the nodes in the memory stack that the learner 'knows' about the notion of local domain. The memory constraint brings about a simulation of this aspect of the grammar, by ensuring that only the local domain is immediately accessible to the memory system.

The general constraints are constraints on how the rules are learned. For example, one general constraint is that children learn language according to the subset principle. According to this principle, children should assume the narrowest possible language that is consistent with the evidence heard so far. The result of this principle is that children will not make any disastrous overgeneralizations. If children did massively overgeneralize, they would never know that they were wrong, because the overgeneralized rule would never be heard in the input and so could not be disconfirmed. This is because the evidence suggests that children do not get corrected for grammatical mistakes (Brown and Hanlon 1970). For example, if the child generalized from

John gave the book to Bill.
John gave Bill the book.

to

John transferred the funds to the bank.
John transferred the bank the funds.

there would be nothing in the input to tell the child that the second overgeneralized rule was wrong. This, of course was one of the problems we encountered with Anderson's computer simulation which relied purely on semantic and cognitive principles.

Another general principle is that children add only one new rule at a time to their grammar. This is in contrast to the traditional hypothesis testing approach which assumed that the children's hypotheses were grammars. Berwick and Weinberg's model assumes that the children's hypotheses are single rules. So, for example, a child will learn the rule of dative movement on encountering

John gave the book to Bill.

and subsequently hearing the sentence containing the moved element:

John gave Bill the book.

But this rule will be specific to the verb *to give*. It will not be generalized to the verb *to transfer* unless the rule was encountered with this verb in the input. Since the child will never encounter an instance of the sentence

John transferred the bank the funds.

the rule of dative movement will never be generated for the verb *transfer*.

This model, then, attempts to account for all of Pinker's conditions for language learning. However, there is still much testing of the model to be done. For example, there seems to have been no attempt to relate the experimental work on pronouns to the output of this computer simulation. It is likely that the model will be subjected to experimental testing on children and that experimental findings other than those on passives will subsequently contribute to the further development of the model.

However, one aspect of language acquisition that is frequently commented upon is that it is a very long drawn out process. Children start off by producing one word at a time and then two words and so on. It is some time after this that they start producing grammatical sentences that might be said to reflect universal grammar. It has sometimes been said that if language is innate, then it should not be acquired so gradually. However, one possible counter-argument to this is that the child is restricted by performance constraints. These may be conceptual in that the child does not possess the concepts to express via language, or to understand particular sentences. Performance constraints may also be due to memory or attentional difficulties. Thus, when children produce one- or two-word utterances, this may have more to do with their memory and attentional spans than with their knowledge of grammar.

A second possible reason for gradual acquisition is that it may be due to maturation of the nervous system. If a biological function has to adapt to a specific environment, then it makes sense to leave a certain amount of latitude for modification. For example, the fine tuning of the binocular cells of the visual system is innately specified but it is also modified by the environment (Blakemore 1978). This fine tuning does not occur until the skull has fully developed and the eyes are in their mature position in the head. Thus the tuning of the cells can take account of whether the eyes are far apart or close together. In a similar way, the development of core grammar (universal grammar with no open parameters) may have to wait until the input from the language community can specify which of many different forms it can take.

Let me mention now, though, one drawback to the approach. This is that it concentrates exclusively on syntax. And if there is one thing that is clear about *performance* (as opposed to competence), it is that people do not understand a sentence purely on the basis of syntax. Pronouns are very good examples of this. For most pronouns, pragmatic inferences have to be used to identify the antecedent. The syntactic constraint that I have described (a pronoun cannot have an antecedent that is higher in the tree in the same local domain) can rule out some possibilities but it cannot always uniquely identify the pronoun. This is shown in the sentence below.

Ann was late for her meeting with Sue and she hurried to get a taxi.

As we have seen before, there are two possible antecedents for the pronoun *she* and they are both in a different clause from the pronoun. So neither of them can be ruled out by the pronominal constraint. Instead, it is necessary to use general knowledge about the possible consequences of being late to infer that *she* refers to Ann. Perhaps the best approach is one which investigates the way in which universal grammar might interact with the child's developing cognitive abilities to enable the child to understand and produce grammatical sentences.

The biggest danger is that history might repeat itself. In the 1960s psychologists adopted transformational grammar as a possible complete account of how language is acquired. This produced a major emphasis on syntax. With the demise of transformational grammar, there was a consequent backlash against the use of transformational grammar in general and models of syntax in particular. Psychologists turned, instead, to models of cognitive or social development for their accounts of language development. The result of this backlash was that syntax was either ignored completely or thought to be acquired on the basis of prior cognitive or social skills. We have seen some problems with these kinds of approaches earlier in the book.

What is needed now is a more measured approach that takes account of both linguistic knowledge, on the one hand, and cognitive and social development, on the other. The study of pronouns would seem to be an ideal testing ground for this approach: they are subject to some of the central constraints of universal grammar, but their interpretation also requires the use of inferences based on general knowledge. Furthermore, there are additional sources of experimental evidence and theoretical perspectives that need to be considered when evaluating Berwick and Weinberg's model. We will consider these experiments and theoretical issues in the next chapter. After that I will take a closer look at the interplay between linguistic and non-linguistic knowledge in the course of development.

Suggested readings

A short account of government binding theory can be found in Chomsky's (1981a) book *Some Concepts and Consequences of the*

Theory of Government and Binding. Additional books on government binding theory are recommended at the end of Chapter 7. Berwick and Weinberg (1984) give a clear account of their computer simulation, and if you would like to find out more about the adult parser of Marcus (1980), his book *A Theory of Syntactic Recognition for Natural Language* is the best source.

CHAPTER 4

Further Developments in Parameter Setting

This chapter is about the kind of work that has been done within the framework of government binding theory and other recent developments in linguistics. All of this work attempts to develop theories of language learning. We will look at a number of different studies which have examined a variety of linguistic structures. The structures we will look at include pronouns, 'complements', relative clauses and passives. We shall see in this work that some very promising ideas are beginning to develop, both about the development of competence and performance and about the nature of the learning mechanism.

Pronouns

As I said in the last chapter, universal grammar consists of a small set of principles (like the notion of local domain and of c-command). But these principles are not completely specified. They contain open parameters. So, for example, the child knows about such structural relations as c-command and local domain. But what the child does not know are the precise rules of pronominal and reflexive interpretation that apply in his/her specific language community. It is exposure to a particular language that specifies how those open parameters are fixed. Once these parameters are fixed, the child has attained the 'core grammar'. Hence acquisition is a process of 'parameter setting'.

So these notions of local domain and c-command are part of universal grammar. What is not specified in the grammar, i.e. what has to be learned, is exactly how these notions constrain (for example) the interpretations of pronouns and reflexives. If you remember, reflexives must have a c-commanding antecedent in the same local domain. Pronouns cannot have a c-commanding antecedent in the same local domain.

One possibility that the child might entertain is that the antecedents of both pronouns and reflexives must always be inside the local domain. That is, the child might assume that the same rule applies to both reflexives and pronouns. There is *some* evidence that children do entertain this possibility (Solan 1983). Young children are more likely to select an antecedent of a pronoun when it is in the same clause (local domain) as the pronoun than when it is in a different clause. Children up to seven years of age make this error but they always interpret reflexives correctly. Thus the reflexive rule seems to be applied not only to reflexives but also to pronouns.

Solan presented children from five to seven years with a selection of toys and asked them to act out certain sentences. Here are the sentences Solan used in one of his experiments.

(1) After he ran around, the horse hit the sheep.
(2) After his run, the horse hit the sheep.

The phrase structure trees for these sentences are shown in Figure 4.1.

In both sentences, the two antecedents are permissible because neither of them c-command the pronoun. However, in sentence (1) the two possible antecedents are not in the same local domain as the pronoun. (Antecedents can come after a pronoun in a sentence as well as before. They just have to conform to the appropriate constraints concerning c-command and local domain.) Thus, in sentence (1) *He ran around* is a separate clause: it is a sentence inside the preposition phrase. So both antecedents are permissible according to two criteria. But in sentence (2), the whole sentence has only one clause (*his run* is a noun phrase, not a separate clause), so both of the possible antecedents are in the same local domain as the pronoun. The question Solan was interested in was whether the children were more likely to select one of the two antecedents in sentence (1) (where they are not in the same local domain) than in sentence (2) (where they are in the same local domain). The alternative would be a toy not mentioned in the sentence.

What Solan found was that the children were more likely to choose either the horse or the sheep when acting out sentence (2) than when

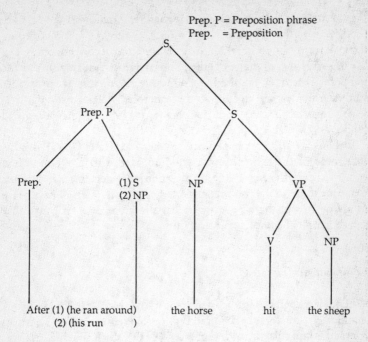

Figure 4.1

acting out sentence (1). With the seven-year olds, for example, 64 per cent chose either the horse or the sheep for sentence (2) but only 36 per cent chose the horse or the sheep for sentence (1). Thus, children are more likely to select an antecedent for a pronoun when both the antecedent and the pronoun are in the same local domain (sentence (2)) than when they are in different local domains (sentence (1)). In other words, the children are acting as if the domain constraint for pronominal interpretation is the same as the domain constraint for reflexive interpretation. In another experiment, the children made no errors when they were presented with sentences containing reflexive pronouns. They always acted out the following sentence correctly.

The dog said that the horse kicked himself.

This supports the proposal that young children assume that antecedents are in the same local domain of both pronouns and reflexives.

Thus, Solan's work provides some support for the view that the children are biologically equipped with knowledge about constraints on possible interpretations. What they are not yet clear about is the way the constraints apply in their own language community. I should add, though, that the evidence is not strong. Sentences (1) and (2) are difficult for reasons other than the interpretation of the pronouns. The use of *before* means that a detailed knowledge of the semantics of the temporal system, is required, for example. And, just as with other studies using *before* and *after*, the sentences violate the pragmatic factors involved in the use of temporal terms (see e.g. Stevenson and Pollitt 1987).

In addition, the work of Deutsch, Koster and Koster (1986) suggests that some of the difficulty that children have with pronouns when compared to reflexives is due to the additional non-linguistic factors that contribute to the comprehension of pronouns. We will have more to say on this in the next chapter. For the moment, I will turn to a consideration of complement structures.

Complement structures

When I described the studies which indicated that a standard transformational grammar is not acquired I contrasted sentences like (1), which contains a null subject, with sentences like (2) which contains an overt subject:

(1) John wants to sing.
(2) John wants Mary to sing.

I pointed out that transformational grammar assumed that sentences like (1) were derived from deep structures like those underlying sentences like (2). Thus, sentence (1) would be transformationally derived from a structure underlying a sentence like (3):

(3) John wants John to sing.

However, government binding theory assumes that sentences like (1) and (2) have *different* d-structures. Sentences with null subjects, like (1), are derived from a structure that contains an empty category. This empty category is called PRO. Thus, the d-structure of (1) is similar to (4):

(4) [John(i) wants [PRO(i) to win]].

where the empty category, PRO, is subject to the same rules of interpretation as personal pronouns. Hence, PRO is interpreted as *John*. This is indicated by the bracketed letters (*i*).

By contrast, the d-structure of (2) is similar to (5):

(5) [John [wants Mary(i) [PRO(i) to sing]]].

In (5), we still have an empty category (PRO), but this time it is interpreted as *Mary*. It is usually assumed that the antecedent of PRO is the nearest c-commanding noun phrase (e.g. Goodluck 1981). The antecedent of PRO is also called the *controller* of PRO.

However, the main point is that there is now no reason to expect sentences containing overt subjects to be easier to acquire than sentences containing null subjects, as was the case with transformational grammar. Instead, they are derived from different d-structures and so would not be expected to have similar courses of development.

In fact, studies have concentrated on investigating the way children understand sentences containing overt subjects. The reason for this is that it allows a test of children's mastery of the notion of c-command. By varying the nature of the sentences, the controller of PRO can be either the subject or the object of the main sentence, *John wants 'something'.* The main sentence is called the matrix sentence. Goodluck (1981) asked children to act out a number of different kinds of sentences. She included sentences with the same form as (2) above e.g.

The boy tells the girl PRO to jump over the fence.

In this sentence, the empty category, PRO, is shown as well. Here, the controller of PRO is the object of the main sentence. However, by using passives, she also included sentences where the controller was the subject of the sentence. For example,

The girl is told by the boy PRO to jump over the fence.

Goodluck found that children as young as four years acted out both kinds of sentences appropriately, a finding which supports a similar observation by Maratsos (1974). Goodluck argued from these findings that four-year olds have knowledge of the structural notion of c-command.

A more recent study by Hsu, Cairns and Fiengo (1985) also investigated a range of sentences containing PRO. They conducted a number of different kinds of studies. First, they collected samples of spontaneous speech; second they asked children to act out the situations described by sentences; and third, they asked the children to say whether the sentences were 'good' or 'silly'. From their observations, they suggest that young children use four different types of grammar before attaining the adult grammar. The first grammar is one that they call a subject–oriented grammar. Children using this grammar invariably interpret PRO as having a subject antecedent. Thus they make mistakes on sentences like

The lion yells at the bear to climb up the ladder.

The children make the lion rather than the bear climb the ladder. Hsu *et al.* suggest that this is a primitive grammar in which the children assume that the subject of the sentence is the subject of all verbs in that sentence. However, the evidence for this particular grammar was not strong.

The second grammar proposed by Hsu *et al.* is one that they called an object-oriented grammar. Children using this grammar invariably interpret PRO as having an object antecedent. Thus they make mistakes with sentences like

The lion pushes the bear after climbing up the ladder.

The children make the bear climb the ladder instead of the lion. Hsu *et al.* take up a proposal first made by Goodluck and suggest that children using this grammar do choose a c-commanding antecedent but have given the wrong structural analysis to the sentence. Goodluck suggested that children initially assume that the preposition phrase is part of the verb phrase instead of the sentence. Thus the children assume a d-structure like (a) in Figure 4.2. instead of one like (b) in the figure.

In (a) but not in (b), the nearest c-commanding noun phrase is *the bear*. *The bear* does not c-command PRO in (b) because its first branching node is the VP and that VP does not dominate the NP which contains PRO. *The lion* does c-command PRO in (b) because the first branching node above the NP containing *the lion* is the S node and this dominates PRO.

The third grammar that Hsu *et al.* propose is called a mixed subject–object grammar. Children who use this grammar are beginning to learn that the preposition phrase in the sentence above is part of the sentence rather than the verb phrase. But incomplete mastery means that these kinds of sentences are sometimes analysed one way and sometimes another.

The fourth type of grammar is called approaching adult grammars. Children using this grammar give the correct interpretations for all the sentences described above, but still make mistakes on sentences where PRO is the first element of the sentence, as in

PRO to have to push the lion scares the bear.

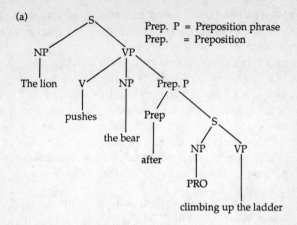

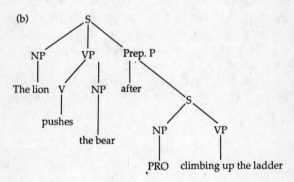

Figure 4.2

Hsu *et al.* found that children interpreted PRO as being some entity not mentioned in the sentence rather than as *the bear*. They follow up a proposal of Tavakolian's (1977) and suggest that this is because children have overgeneralized the c-command constraint and so will not interpret PRO as having a controller that does not c-command it. Thus Hsu *et al.* argue that children use a series of grammars that are based on the structure of the sentence and the notion of c-command. In doing so, they describe a number of developmental stages in the framework of government binding theory.

However, there are a number of difficulties with this study. First, it is not really consistent with the findings of Goodluck (1981) and Maratsos (1974) that I described earlier. Goodluck and Maratsos found that children could understand both subject controlled and object controlled sentences. But this should not occur if they are using one of the four grammars described by Hsu *et al*. Second, it is purely descriptive and does not attempt to explain how a child moves from one grammar to another. Indeed, it is not at all clear why children should use four intermediate grammars before they use the adult form. Nothing in government binding theory or in the notion of learning by parameter setting would lead to such an expectation. Third, Hsu *et al*. use a mixture of techniques and some, such as acting out and spontaneous speech, measure performance while the sentence judgement task measures competence. But they do not attempt to distinguish between competence and performance.

Furthermore, government binding theory and parameter setting make no predictions about the relative difficulties of the different types of structures that they observe. For example, it is not clear what parameters are left open initially, nor how they change once they have been fixed and have produced an intermediate grammar. Basically, the study does not address the issue of learnability. What is clear is that processing or performance factors need to be disentangled from questions of competence – as I have argued before. In the next section I will describe a study which examines the acquisition of relative clauses but which also attempts to distinguish between competence and performance.

Relative clauses

Sentences which contain relative clauses are complex sentences that have received a lot of attention from developmental psycholinguists. An example of such a sentence is

The lion kisses the duck that hits the pig.

A tree diagram of the sentence is shown in Figure 4.3.

The relative clause is *e hits the pig* and it is embedded in a matrix sentence: *The lion kisses the duck*. The relative clause says something more about the object of this matrix sentence (*the duck*), and the empty category (*e*) in the relative clause is the subject of the clause. For these reasons, the relative clause is called an object–subject (OS) relative.

In government binding theory, it is widely accepted that the empty NP position in a relative clause must not be higher in the tree than the noun phrase that it refers to. Thus, the interpretation of the empty

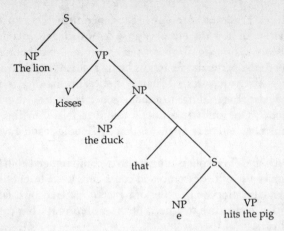

Figure 4.3

noun phrase is subject to a c-command condition: the antecedent of an empty noun phrase must c-command the empty noun phrase. This means that the empty noun phrase in the tree diagram above is interpreted as being *the duck*. (It is usually assumed that the nearest c-commanding noun phrase is the antecedent.)

However, much of the work on the acquisition of relative clauses has been carried out prior to the development of government binding theory and the resulting findings have been interpreted in a number of different ways. For example, a number of people have found that when children are asked to act out the situations described by sentences containing relative clauses, performance is rather poor with object–subject relatives.

This finding has been interpreted by Sheldon (1974) as indicating that children use a parallel function strategy. They interpret the empty noun phrase in the relative clause as having an antecedent that fills the same grammatical role in the matrix sentence. The subject of the matrix sentence (*the lion*) is assumed to be the antecedent of the empty category *e*. Thus in the OS sentence above, children interpret the sentence to mean that the lion hits the pig. On the other hand, Tavakolian (1981) has suggested that what the children are doing is interpreting the sentences containing relative clauses in the same way as sentences which consist of conjoined sentences. Thus Tavakolian suggests that children interpret OS relatives as if they were sentences like *The lion kisses the pig and the lion jumps over the fence*.

The trouble with these interpretations is that they give an account only of what the children are doing in the experiment. They do not give an explanation of how the mistakes arise or of their role in a developmental theory. They are also very piecemeal accounts because they apply only to the particular sentences being studied (in this case those containing relative clauses). What is noticeably lacking is a clear attempt to relate the findings to either a general competence or performance model. One study that does attempt to relate the findings to both competence and performance is that by Goodluck and Tavakolian (1982).

Goodluck and Tavakolian propose that children aged four to five years do make use of the c-command constraint at the level of competence. They also propose that performance is affected by a language processor that is sensitive to aspects of the sentence which increase the memory load.

We will look first at some of the evidence that they use to support the notion that children have a knowledge of c-command. In their second experiment, Goodluck and Tavakolian examined children's comprehension of sentences containing OS relatives. However, they varied the form of the sentences so that some were active and others were passive. An example of an active sentence is:

The boy hits the girl that jumps over the fence.

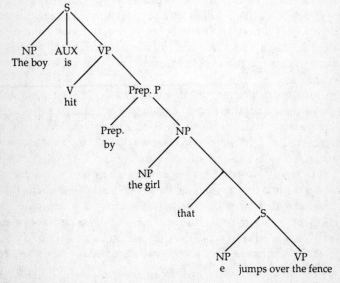

Figure 4.4

The tree structure for a sentence similar to this was shown in Figure 4.3. An example of a passive sentence is

The boy is hit by the girl that jumps over the fence.

This sentence has the tree structure shown in Figure 4.4.

In both of these examples, the antecedent of the empty noun phrase is the nearest c-commanding noun phrase – *the girl* in both cases. The children acted out sentences like these with this correct interpretation nearly 60 per cent of the time and the performance was similar for both kinds of sentences. However, Goodluck and Tavokolian also included sentences that contained temporal complements. An example of an active sentence containing a temporal complement is

The boy hits the girl after jumping the fence.

This has the tree structure shown in Figure 4.5.

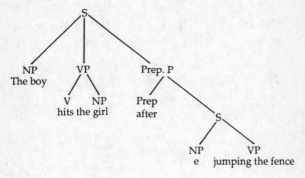

Figure 4.5

In this sentence, the only c-commanding NP is *the boy*. So the empty noun phrase (*e*) is interpreted as *the boy*. *The girl* does not c-command *e* because its first branching node is VP and the VP does not dominate *e*.

A similar analysis applies to a passive sentence containing a temporal complement. An example is

The boy is hit by the girl after jumping the fence.

The tree structure for this sentence is shown in Figure 4.6.

Again, the nearest noun phrase that c-commands the empty NP is *the boy*.

However, Goodluck and Tavakolian argue that young children have not yet learned the relevant structural position of the temporal

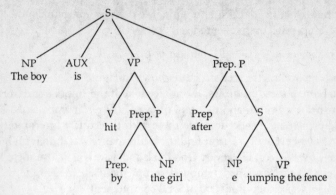

Figure 4.6

complement and that they frequently assign it to the verb phrase node rather than to the sentence node. This would result in the tree structures shown in Figure 4.7 for the active and passive sentences respectively.

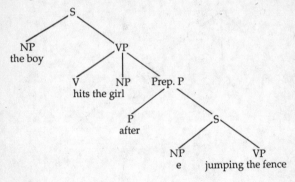

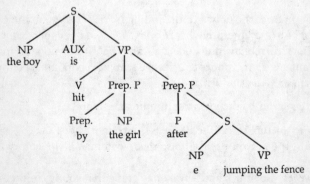

Figure 4.7

If we look at these tree structures, we can see that the nearest noun phrase that c-commands the empty noun phrase is now *the girl* in the active sentence. But it is still *the boy* in the passive sentence. The results showed that the children interpreted the temporal complement as referring to *the girl* 52 per cent of the time with the active sentences, but only 25 per cent of the time with the passive sentences. Thus Goodluck and Tavakolian argue that this supports their proposal that the children give an incorrect structural assignment to these sentences, but still maintain the c-command constraint. The fact that performance is never 100 per cent is attributed to the second feature highlighted by Goodluck and Tavakolian.

This is that the sentence processor is affected by features of the sentence that affect memory load. For example, children find sentences with animate direct objects more difficult to process than sentences with inanimate direct objects. They showed that this was the case in their first experiment where they asked children to act out the situations described by sentences containing relative clauses. Again, OS relatives were used, but they contained either an animate object e.g.

The dog kicks the horse that knocks over the sheep.

or an inanimate object:

The dog kicks the horse that knocks over the table.

They found that children were much more likely to act out the sentence correctly when the relative clause contained an inanimate object than when it contained an animate object. Goodluck and Tavakolian explain this additional difficulty with an animate object in terms of a particular processing model of language. I will describe the processing model first, and then show how Goodluck and Tavakolian use this model to explain the children's difficulties with an animate object.

The model of a sentence processor that they use is one proposed by Frazier and Fodor (1978). Briefly, Frazier and Fodor propose that there are two stages involved in processing (or parsing) a sentence. In the first stage, the processor analyses a restricted range of words as they are heard and attempts to build up a syntactic structure for these words without regard for the overall structure of the sentence being analysed. The limits on this stage are limits on the capacity of working memory. It is likely that this capacity is limited by features such as time and number of words as well as by structural complexity. Once the capacity of working memory is exceeded, the least current material is passed to the second stage of the parser. In this second stage, the processor can complete the analysis and can revise it in the light of the overall structure of the sentence that has been constructed so far.

Goodluck and Tavakolian suggest that children can analyse the complete relative clause when it contains an inanimate object in the first parsing stage. This allows the empty noun phrase to be attached to the correct antecedent because it is still in working memory. However, they suggest that an animate object in the relative clause adds sufficient additional difficulty for working memory to be overloaded so that the matrix sentence is passed to the second stage before the empty noun phrase can be attached to the c-commanding noun phrase. This means that the relative clause has no potential antecedent in the first stage and so can be interpreted only in the second stage. They also propose that in the second stage the children are more likely to attach the relative clause to the sentence node than to the NP node. If they do this, then the only c-commanding noun phrase of the empty category is the subject of the sentence. Hence, the children make more (subject) errors when relative clauses contain animate as opposed to inanimate objects.

These proposals by Goodluck and Tavakolian are only tentative. But they do show how it is possible to develop an account of language development that considers both competence and performance. As they point out, and as I have tried to argue earlier in this book, the data from studies of children's language are performance data which may reflect competence only indirectly. Goodluck and Tavakolian show how a close analysis of performance data can be used to tease out features of universal grammar (competence) and features of the language processor (performance). They are able to do this because of two things. First, they have well specified models of the adult system – current syntactic theory for a model of competence and the approach of Frazier and Fodor for a model of performance. Second, they use a variety of sentence types in the same experiments. The examples I gave were relative clauses and temporal complements, but they included another kind of sentence as well. It is by seeing how the same children perform on a range of sentences with different structures that it becomes possible to infer the underlying competence of the children and to distinguish aspects of competence from aspects of performance.

This study suggests that the way forward for understanding children's developing competence as well as performance is by using a number of different sentence constructions on the same children. However, another approach is to examine the way that children will generalize a rule when faced with a novel word. That approach has been used extensively by Pinker and his colleagues (e.g. Pinker, Lebeaux and Frost 1987) to study the acquisition of the passive rule. We will discuss this approach in the next section.

Passive sentences

The passive construction has been a major challenge both to accounts of development based on transformational grammar and to grammatical theory itself. Children's use of the passive transformation was an example of the failure of the standard transformational grammar to account for language development. The standard 1965 model of transformational grammar required the application of four different kinds of transformational rule to derive the surface structure from the deep structure. This variety of rules was specific to passive sentences and did not provide an explanatory account of different kinds of sentences. However, government binding theory uses a small set of interacting principles to explain how some sentences were grammatical while others were not, regardless of the particular sentence construction. The passive construction, for example, makes use of the notion of case and empty categories.

However, there is one feature of passive constructions that remains a challenge to both linguists and developmental psycholinguists. This feature was originally highlighted by Baker (1979). It is a fact that the passive rule does not apply to all verbs. So how do children learn which verbs can occur in passive sentences and which cannot? Baker pointed out that, for a wide range of constructions, there is no obvious relationship between verbs that occur in those constructions and verbs that do not. The passive construction is one example of this general case where it has proved particularly difficult to specify exactly what characterizes verbs that can occur in the passive form and verbs that cannot. Quite the contrary, in fact. For example, the passive construction involves transitive verbs in English; but not all transitive verbs can occur in the passive form, as the following examples show:

(1) The argument escapes many people.
    This bottle contains a deadly poison.
    John has three bicycles.

(2) Many people are escaped by the argument.
    A deadly poison is contained by the bottle.
    Three bicycles are had by John.

These examples come from Pinker *et al.* (1987) and they show that the passive versions in (2) are not grammatical. The problem then, is how children do not massively overgeneralize once they discover passive sentences in the language. Baker's solution to this problem (which he showed occurred for a variety of sentence types) was to propose that children are conservative learners. They use verbs in their passive form only if they have already heard them in the passive. Thus, the lexical information in the verbs is learned separately for each verb. For some time, this appeared to be the only solution to the problem, and indeed, Baker's paper played a crucial role in constraining the power of models of grammar. In particular he reminded linguists of the need for grammatical theory to be learnable by a child.

However, if this is the way that children learn passive (among other) constructions, then it makes the learning process a very protracted one. Not only that, it implies that children will use passives only with verbs that they have encountered in the passive form. But this does not seem to be the case. A number of researchers have observed that children do use passives productively. That is, they use passives with verbs that they would not have heard in the passive form. For example, Bowerman (1983) reported one of her daughters saying *If you don't put them in for a very long time they won't get staled*, referring to crackers in a bread box. Pinker *et al.* give other examples from Adam, Eve and Sarah (the children studied by Brown 1973a) and from other sources.

Given these observations, the problem is not solved, because we still need to know how children grow up to recognize that a sentence like *Three bicycles are had by John* is ungrammatical. The problem seems to have become more difficult with these examples of productivity, not easier. Pinker *et al.* made up novel words to examine how far children from three- to eight-years old will use them in the passive form when they have not heard them in that form. In particular, Pinker *et al.* created novel words of particular kinds to test a number of possibilities of how passive verbs might form a coherent set.

For example, Pinker (1982) has suggested that initially children apply the rule only to subjects and objects that are agents and patients respectively. Pinker refers to this as the 'semantic bootstrapping hypothesis'. That is, children do use syntactic rather than semantic categories (unlike the meaning view discussed in Chapter 2), but they use semantic information to constrain the domain of application of a rule such as passive. In the case of the passive, by restricting the rule to subjects and objects that are agents and patients the child is able to form some generalizations (to other agent–patient sequences) rather than learning verb by verb. There is evidence to suggest that children comprehend passives containing action verbs, like *hit*, more readily than they do passives containing perception verbs, like *see*, and it is action verbs that express agent–patient relationships (e.g. Maratsos, Kuczaj, Fox and Chalkley 1979). In addition, such a generalization is possible because all agent–patient verbs do passivize. On the other hand, this is not the correct adult rule, so at some stage the child has to learn that other subject–object combinations can be passivized. Possibly this is done on a verb by verb basis.

Pinker *et al*. tested this possibility by creating four novel verbs, two of them action verbs and two of them perception verbs. For example, the non-word *gump* might be used to express the action 'to rub the back of the neck of', while the non-word *pell* might be used to express the perceptual relationship 'to hear through an ear-trumpet-like instrument'. Children were then taught the meanings of these non-words in either the active or the passive form. For example, they would be shown two dolls acting together and would hear the sentence *The dog is gumping the elephant*. Other children would only hear the passive version, *The elephant is being gumped by the dog*. The same procedure was used for the novel perception verbs. The children were then tested on their ability to produce sentences containing these non-words in either the active or the passive form. They were required to describe the actions of the dolls themselves.

To encourage the children to use the active voice they would be prompted with *Here's the (eg) dog. The dog is doing something to the elephant. What is happening?* To encourage the children to use the passive voice, the child was prompted with *Here's the (eg) elephant. Nothing's happening to the elephant. Now something's going to happen to the elephant. I want you to tell me what's happening*. Then the experimenter made the dolls act out the meaning of the non-word and the child described it.

The critical results were those cases where the child learned the active version and was encouraged to produce a passive version of the same verb. These are cases of productivity. The child has generalized from the active to the passive form without ever hearing the verb in its passive form. What Pinker *et al*. found in these cases was that the children were just as likely to passivize the perception verbs as they were to passivize the action verbs. Thus, the suggestion that children confine the passive rule to action verbs was not supported. This finding was confirmed in a second study where the non-words described either actions or static spatial relationships. Here, too, the children were just as likely to generalize from the active to the passive with spatial verbs as they were with action verbs. It appears, therefore, that children are not conservative learners and that they generalize the passive to new verbs even when they have not heard them in the passive and even when the verbs describe non-actions.

What Pinker *et al.* propose, therefore, is that children generalize on the basis of the argument structure of the verb. (Pinker *et al.*'s account is based on Bresnan's (1978) lexical functional grammar. However, it is not incompatible with government binding theory, so I will describe their ideas from the point of view of the latter theory.) Specifically, Pinker *et al.* propose that the thematic roles associated with each verb determine whether the verb can be passivized. They argue that universal grammar specifies that verbs which can be passivized are those where the underlying subject argument has an agent thematic role and the underlying object argument has a patient thematic role.

In support of this proposal, Pinker *et al.* carried out a third study where the non-words described actions which violated this argument structure. For example, they used the non-word *flooze*, in which the argument structure consisted of a theme (or patient) in the subject position and of an agent in the object position. Thus the sentence *The dog floozed the giraffe* meant that the giraffe leapfrogged over the dog. These 'anticanonical' verbs were contrasted with canonical verbs where the agent was the subject and the patient was the object. In this study, Pinker *et al.* found that the children were extremely reluctant to passivize the anticanonical verbs when they had only heard them in the active form. This was in contrast to their willingness to passivize canonical verbs in the same situation and to passivize non-action verbs in the previous studies.

Thus, there is some support for this notion that children restrict their use of passives to verbs with agent subjects and patient objects. However, as Pinker *et al.* point out, this does not account for the full range of passives that are possible in English. Neither perception verbs nor spatial verbs could be passivized if this was an absolute rule. Yet children readily passivize such verbs, and these verbs can be passivized in English. Pinker *et al.* suggest, therefore, that languages vary in the way that these agent–patient thematic roles can be extended to include verbs that do not obviously have this argument structure.

In particular, English defines a large class of verbs that can be interpreted as having an agent–patient argument structure only at an abstract level. For example, some spatial verbs in English are not passivizable at all. These are verbs like *lack* which cannot be interpreted as having a patient argument. The thing that is contained is not affected by the container in any way. By contrast, some spatial verbs can be passivized. These are verbs like *surround* or *lined*. For example,

The house was surrounded by a moat.
The street was lined by trees.

It turns out that these verbs can also be used in a sense where the object is affected by the action and hence can be regarded at one level as having a patient in object position. This can be seen from the following examples.

The landscapers surrounded the house with a lawn.
The planner lined the street with trees.

On the basis of these observations, Pinker *et al*. suggest that these 'abstract' agent–patient verbs have to be learned by young children because the particular range of verbs that can be used in this way is specific to English. However, Pinker also argues that once the child has learned the way the agent–patient verbs can be extended in the language, then the passive rule can be used productively. It can be applied to verbs that have not been heard in the passive form. Thus, Pinker proposes a way out of the problem originally posed by Baker (1979). Children are not conservative learners. Instead, they generalize initially on the basis of 'canonical' agent–patient verbs (the action verbs) but rapidly learn the way that these pure agent–patient verbs can be extended to other verbs in the language so that these other verbs can then also be passivized.

This work of Pinker's is an impressive example of the way that questions of learnability and linguistic theory can be used to help us understand how children learn language. Again, the details of his proposals have not been confirmed, but they show how the puzzle of language development may yet be understood. They also indicate that a model such as Berwick and Weinberg's may need to take account not only of case theory but also of the argument structure of the verbs, particularly the thematic roles that fill those arguments, if a full account of how passives are learned is to be given.

In fact all the work described in this chapter contributes in different ways to our understanding of language learning. It is sometimes said that the proposal of an innate language mechanism removes the need to explain the learning process. I hope I have shown in this chapter and the previous one that an innate language mechanism does not remove the need for explaining how language is learned. Indeed, it seems that it is only by making this assumption that any specific proposals concerning learning can be made.

Suggested readings

Perhaps the best reference source for recent work based on current linguistic theory is the book edited by Roeper and Williams called *Parameter Setting*. The journal *Cognition* also publishes a number of articles on language learning. It is worthwhile looking through that journal for relevant articles. Pinker's work is based on Joan Bresnan's grammar, which is discussed in her book called *The Mental Representation of Grammatical Relations*. Pinker also has a chapter in that book, which gives an account of his views on language learning. Pinker's (1984) own book, *Language Learnability and Language Development* gives a fuller treatment of his views.

CHAPTER 5

The Acquisition of Pronouns

On a number of occasions now I have referred to the fact that pronouns cannot be comprehended purely on the basis of linguistic knowledge. Indeed, I started this book with the example of pronouns to make this point about language development in general. In this chapter, therefore, I will discuss the work on pronouns in more detail. In particular, I hope to show how we need to draw on all three of the knowledge sources involved in language – social, cognitive and linguistic – in order to use language appropriately. To set the scene, I will demonstrate the roles of these knowledge sources.

The social knowledge required to use pronouns is an understanding of interpersonal roles. In a conversation we can identify three different roles: the speaker, the listener and the non-participants. The role that different individuals fill will vary over time. For example, in a group of people, I will be a speaker at one moment and I will be speaking to one or several people. So there will be one or more listeners while I am speaking. If I am speaking to a particular individual, then there will be other members of the group who are non-participants. They are neither speakers nor listeners. At some other moment, another individual may be speaking. If he or she is speaking to me then I am now in the listener role, but if he or she is speaking to someone else then I will be a non-participant. It is these roles that determine which pronoun will be used. The speaker is identified by the pronoun *I*, the listener is identified

by the pronoun *you*, and non-participants are identified by the pronouns *he* or *she* (if only one individual is being referred to), or *they* (if
several people are being referred to). Knowledge of these roles, and
how they may change, is crucial for very young children when they
begin to use pronouns. A child must realize that when the mother uses *I*
to identify herself and *you* to identify the child, she is referring to roles,
not to particular individuals. Thus, when the child speaks, he or she
must realize that *I* now identifies himself and not his/her mother, and
you now identifies the mother and not him/herself. Similarly, when a
third person is being referred to *he* or *she* will be used. And if that third
person becomes the speaker, then either the mother or the child can be
identified by one of these third person pronouns. An understanding of
these roles and the way they are identified by different pronouns is a
very complex skill which young children acquire.

Linguistic knowledge is also required for the appropriate use of the
pronouns. Such knowledge is basically of two kinds: lexical knowledge
and structural knowledge. Lexical knowledge refers to information in
the word itself. One kind of lexical information is knowledge of person
(or role). *I* is in the first person and identifies the speaker, *she* is in the
third person and identifies a non-participant. A second kind of information is knowledge of number (one person or more than one). *She* is
singular, *they* is plural. Finally, a third kind of lexical information is
gender, e.g. *he* versus *she*.

Structural knowledge concerns constraints on the interpretation of
pronouns. I have already discussed the constraint on pronominal interpretation and will mention it again very briefly. Consider again the
sentence below.

John said that Bill liked him.

As I pointed out before, if there were no grammar (i.e. no structural
constraints on interpretation), then in principle either *John* or *Bill*
could be antecedents of *him*. However, the grammar specifies a constraint on what can be a permissible antecedent for a pronoun. This
constraint is that a pronoun cannot have an antecedent that is higher up
in the phrase structure tree than the pronoun and that is in (roughly)
the same clause as the pronoun. If the antecedent is higher in the phrase
structure tree than the pronoun, the antecedent is said to c-command
the pronoun. Thus a pronoun cannot have a c-commanding antecedent
that is in the same clause as the pronoun. So in the sentence above,
there is only one possible antecedent for *him*, namely, *John*. *Bill* cannot
be an antecedent because it is in the same clause (or local domain) as the

pronoun. (See Chapter 7 for further details.) Thus, this structural constraint rules out certain potential antecedents as impermissible. Again, young children (as well as adults) need to use this knowledge both to produce and understand pronouns appropriately.

I should point out that this structural knowledge is also quite distinct from the knowledge of social roles described above. In the example sentence, the pronoun refers to an individual who has already been mentioned in the sentence. That is, the pronoun has an antecedent in the sentence itself. By contrast, when I was talking about social roles, I was talking about how a pronoun identified an individual in the conversation. The pronoun was used to point to a person who occupied a particular role in the actual physical situation itself. We can thus make a distinction between pronouns which point directly to an individual in the world, and which make maximum use of our knowledge of social roles, and pronouns which refer to an individual who is not necessarily present in the situation but has been introduced in an earlier utterance. In this latter case, we can identify the individual only by locating the earlier reference in the utterance. And this is the process that the structural constraint applies to. Pronouns which point directly to an individual in the world are known as 'deictic' pronouns, while pronouns that refer to individuals introduced in a prior utterance are known as 'anaphoric' pronouns.

Cognitive information is obviously involved in the use of both these kinds of pronouns. Deictic pronouns such as *I* and *you* involve the concepts of self and other as well as a knowledge of social roles. However, it is anaphoric pronouns which have received most attention where cognitive information is concerned. This is because linguistic information, either lexical or structural, is not sufficient to interpret all examples of pronouns. Take this sentence, for example:

> Jane was late for her appointment with Sue and she hurried to get a taxi.

In this sentence, linguistic knowledge is insufficient to interpret the pronoun, *she*. Thus, neither *Jane* nor *Sue* can be ruled out as potential antecedents on linguistic grounds. The lexical information (third person, singular, feminine) is compatible with both these potential antecedents, and the structural information is also unable to rule out either *Jane* or *Sue* as permissible antecedents. The pronoun is contained in an independent clause, so the structural constraint, that a pronoun cannot have a c-commanding antecedent in the same local domain (or clause) does not apply at all. The sentence, therefore, is linguistically ambiguous. However, there is a sense in which the pronoun is not really ambiguous at all. This is because we are able to make pragmatic inferences, or inferences derived from our general knowledge, about some possible consequences of being late to infer that *she* refers to *Jane*. Thus, we interpret the pronoun by means of inferences from our non-linguistic general knowledge store, and not by means of linguistic knowledge. This sentence cannot be explained by a more simple heuristic strategy such as 'assign the pronoun to the subject of the sentence', as the following example shows:

Joan lent the book to Mary and she forgot to return it.

Here, we infer that *she* refers to *Mary* who is the object of the sentence.

We have seen, then, that pronouns can be of two kinds: deictic and anaphoric. We have also seen that to be able to use pronouns appropriately requires the use not only of linguistic knowledge but also of non-linguistic knowledge, both social and cognitive. Thus for the developing child, pronouns present a challenging task. Their acquisition will depend not only on the availability of these different concepts and skills, but also on the child's ability to integrate the different skills and bring them all to bear on the task of producing or understanding pronouns. It is time, then, to consider the work on the acquisition of pronouns.

Several points will emerge as this discussion progresses. One is that work in this field is fragmentary. People study either deictic or anaphoric pronouns, but never the two together. The development of deictic pronouns is analysed either from a social point of view or from a linguistic (lexical) point of view, but never both. Similarly, the development of anaphoric pronouns is considered either from a purely structural view or from a cognitive view, but structural and cognitive aspects are never considered together. Finally, the cognitive aspects themselves tend to be investigated from one of two points of view.

In general, investigators concentrate either on the use of pragmatic inferences of the kind described above or on thematic aspects of the narrative, such as a distinction between main and subsidiary characters. A second point is that when pragmatic inferences are studied, no attempt is made to manipulate directly the ease with which such inferences can be made: there is little attempt to relate the work to more general principles of the child's developing cognitive skills. A third point is that each study tends to use a different task. This makes it difficult to equate the findings from different studies. A fourth point is that many of the tasks are very difficult for young children to carry out, thus making the findings very tentative, and a fifth point (which should be obvious by now) is that there are still many gaps in our understanding of the acquisition of pronouns, both in the way the use of a particular knowledge source emerges and in the way the different knowledge sources interact.

Deictic pronouns

It is generally maintained that deictic pronouns are logically prior to anaphoric pronouns in their use (Lyons 1977). Lyons has also argued that the deictic use appears earlier than the anaphoric. That is, children will initially use pronouns to refer to things that are physically present in the context rather than ones that refer to an individual known only by prior mention in the utterance. From a psychological point of view, such a position makes sense. A deictic pronoun can refer to the world directly; it does not require the use of some form of internal representation. By contrast, anaphoric pronouns can be used and understood only if some form of internal representation is available from which to retrieve information about the antecedent. It is only through the antecedent that an anaphoric pronoun can be interpreted. However, the two types of pronouns have rarely been investigated in a single study. When they are the results seem to suggest that the basics of both third person deictic and third person anaphoric forms are mastered by the age of three (Webster and Ingram 1972).

Webster and Ingram asked children aged between 3.0 and 4.5 years to act out sentences of three levels of complexity. The simplest form contained a single deictic pronoun (*She is sleeping*). A second type used two deictic pronouns (*She is pushing him*). And the most complex contained two anaphoric pronouns (*The father chases the girl and now he is tickling her*). Thus, this study used only third person pronouns, not first or second person ones. In addition, the sentences containing anaphoric pronouns were predictable given the context, and many studies have found that children will use their knowledge of probable events in the world (rather than their knowledge of language) to act out sentences using toys. Strohner and Nelson (1974), for example, suggest that children seem to use a probable event strategy to do predictable things with toy objects when they do not understand the experimenter.

Studies that have investigated young children's use of *I* and *you* as well as *he* and *she* have concentrated on the deictic forms (Brener 1983, Charney 1980). Brener showed children video scenes containing four individuals. A comprehension question was asked about each scene. For example, in one scene the speaker addressed the sentence *She drank the milk* to a listener in the presence of two participants. The child was then asked to point to the individual he or she thought the pronoun referred to. Charney examined both production and comprehension. In the comprehension task, the children were presented with three colour photographs, one of the child, one of his/her mother, and one of the experimenter. The experimenter then hid a toy under one of the photographs and said *It's under my/your/her picture*. This was addressed to either the child or the mother and in both cases the child was required to get the toy.

The basic finding from these studies is that very young children from 1.6 up to 5.6 acquire the use of *I* first, quickly followed by *you* and only later do they use *he* or *she* appropriately. Charney has used such data to propose that young children learn these pronouns initially from the point of view of their own role as speakers. Thus *I* is acquired before *you*. Deutsch and Pechman (1978), studying German children, propose that the speaker–listener relationship is particularly salient for young children; hence *I* and *you* are acquired before third person references. However, Deutsch and Pechman explain their findings in terms of the complexity of linguistic contrasts rather than in terms of the salience of the child's social role. It is difficult on the basis of the data to distinguish between these two views.

However, Scholes (1981) presents data that might favour the former view: that children's difficulties lie not with the notion of social roles but with the particular lexical items associated with these roles. He found that children from the age of five can distinguish third person pronouns on the basis of gender (*he* v *she*), followed by distinctions on the basis of number (*he* v *they*) and case (*he* v *him*). This latter distinction is related to grammatical not social role, suggesting that it is the linguistic features that are slowly acquired, not the knowledge of social roles. One problem with this study, though, is that it required the children to match sentences containing pronouns to black and white line drawings. The drawings themselves are very confusable, so the task itself might have contributed to the children's performance. More recently, Pinker (1982, Chapter 5) has proposed a model of language acquisition which seems to predict that number should be acquired before gender, so a more detailed look at this issue is clearly required.

This brief survey of work on deictic pronouns leaves many questions unanswered. The basic finding seems to be that *I* is acquired before *you*, and both of these are acquired before *he* or *she*. The problem with this basic observation, though, is that none of the studies cited used adult controls. And yet we might expect that adults too would have difficulty with third person deictic pronouns. It is difficult to refer to a non-participant in a small group by using *he* or *she*. In addition, it is difficult to find suitable tasks to present to children as young as 1.6 years of age that can adequately reflect their linguistic abilities, rather than the cognitive demands of the task itself. Thus, the only firm conclusion that can be drawn here is that by the age of three children have begun to use deictic pronouns. What remains unknown is the full extent of this ability, whether it is really the case that deictic pronouns are acquired before anaphoric pronouns, and what aspects of the pronominal system resist acquisition until a later stage.

Anaphoric pronouns

Structural constraints

At the beginning of this chapter, I illustrated Chomsky's (1981) pronominal constraint with the following sentence:

John said that Bill liked him.

I pointed out that *Bill* could not be the antecedent of the pronoun *him*, because it violated the pronominal constraint: *Bill* is in the same local domain as the pronoun, and it also c-commands the pronoun. Indeed, if we wished to say that Bill liked Bill, then we would have used the reflexive pronoun *himself* instead. Thus, the constraint on the interpretation of reflexive pronouns seems to be the mirror image of that for personal pronouns like *him*: a reflexive pronoun must have a c-commanding antecedent in the same local domain.

As we saw in the last chapter, these notions of c-command and local domain are regarded by Chomsky as part of universal grammar. In the last chapter, I also pointed out that Solan (1983) had presented evidence to suggest that children seemed to have knowledge of the universal principle 'local domain' but that at first they misapplied it. According to Solan, children up to the age of seven interpret personal pronouns as if they must have an antecedent in the same local domain. In other words they interpret these pronouns as if they were reflexives. The critical point, though, is that they do make use of the structural principle 'local domain'. What they seem not yet to have learned is how to apply this principle appropriately. In another experiment, Solan argues that children from the age of five make use of the notion c-command to interpret pronouns. The subject of a sentence is always higher in the phrase structure tree than anything else in the sentence. Thus the subject c-commands everything else in the sentence. In particular, the subject of a sentence c-commands the object of that sentence, as shown in Figure 5.1.

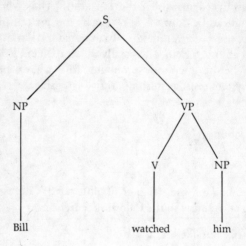

Figure 5.1

In this sentence the subject, *Bill*, c-commands the object, *him*, but *him* does not c-command *Bill*. Solan found that young children were much more likely to act out a sentence if a pronoun in object position had a subject antecedent; but if the sentence had a pronoun in the *subject* position, as in *He watched Bill*, the children were much more likely to interpret the pronoun as if it referred to something outside the sentence. Thus, Solan argued that the children were sensitive to the structural notion of c-command (even though it meant that the object pronouns were wrongly interpreted). Unfortunately, Solan's sentences in this experiment were extremely difficult. Two examples are given below:

The horse hit him in the sheep's yard.

He hit the horse in the sheep's yard.

It is unclear how adults would interpret sentences like these, so Solan's findings remain very speculative. Since the notion of c-command plays such a central role in Chomsky's (1981) theory of government and binding, it would seem crucial to test children's command of the notion with simpler sentences. It may be, for example, that children do apply the pronominal constraint appropriately if other aspects of the task are not too demanding. In fact, given the difficulty of Solan's sentences, it is striking that even so the children indicated an understanding of c-command.

However, even if children are biologically equipped with such structural notions as 'local domain' and c-command, they still have to learn how these notions apply in their particular language community. For example, some languages have a slightly different constraint on the interpretation of personal pronouns. Malayalam and Chinese, for instance, have an absolute ban on pronouns preceding their antecedents (Mohanan 1981). This is not the case in English, as the following example shows:

Before he entered the room, John straightened his tie.

Here the pronoun *he* precedes its antecedent *John*. The child, then, must learn exactly how the structural principles apply in his/her own language community.

Some people (e.g. Lust 1981, Tavakolian 1978) have suggested that young children first assume an absolute ban on pronouns preceding their antecedents. Thus, Lust has found that children up to the age of about four fail to imitate sentences like the one above correctly. However, they can correctly imitate sentences like

Before John entered the room he straightened his tie.

Thus it is possible that children start off with a constraint that is too restrictive.

Again, this survey of studies concerned with structural constraints has been brief. But the most striking observation is that these linguistic principles have been investigated quite independently of other aspects of the use of pronouns. For example, children's general cognitive abilities are developing at this time. Yet we do not know which skills are the first to emerge, for example. I shall say more about this when I have discussed the studies which investigate cognitive aspects of pronoun use. For the moment, it should be noted that the evidence for a knowledge of structural constraints such as c-command and 'local domain' is not strong. This is because it is difficult to compose sentences which vary the need for these constraints and which are simple enough to impose no other irrelevant cognitive demands on the child. Hence the studies that have been conducted are difficult to interpret. The possibility does remain, though, that very young children start off with a rule which says that pronouns cannot precede their antecedents, a rule which must subsequently be rejected for the correct one. (But see Goodluck 1986, for conflicting evidence.) Similarly, it seems to be the case that young children understand the constraints on the interpretation of reflexive pronouns before they can grasp the constraints on the interpretation of anaphoric pronouns. (But again there are conflicting results, see Matthei 1981.)

Children's use of pragmatic inferences

There seem to have been only three studies that have explicitly investigated children's use of pragmatic inferences while interpreting pronouns. These are the studies of Tyler (1983), Tyler and Marslen-Wilson (1982) and Wykes (1981). As we shall see, these studies do not produce consistent findings, but before we examine them further, it is appropriate here to consider the notion of inferences in more detail. Earlier in this chapter, I gave the following example of the use of inferences:

> Jane was late for her appointment with Sue and she hurried to get a taxi.

I pointed out that, despite the linguistic ambiguity of the pronoun, the sentences can be interpreted by means of inferences based on our general knowledge of the world. We know that if someone is late they are likely to hurry. Hence we can infer that *she* refers to *Jane*.

The development of inferential abilities

The ability of young children to make inferences has been a matter of some debate, particularly in the Piagetian literature. Piaget has claimed that children are unable to make abstract inferences (i.e. inferences based on knowledge derived from sentences) until the formal operational stage at the age of about ten to eleven. He has also claimed that children are unable to make inferences at all until the concrete operational stage at about seven years of age. It is only at this stage, for example, that young children can use the notion of transitive inference to sort a set of differently sized sticks into an order corresponding to their increasing size.

According to Piaget, this is because it is only at the concrete operational stage of development that young children are able to use the operation of reciprocity. This operation is the ability to recognize reciprocal relations. Thus if stick A is smaller than stick B and stick B is smaller than stick C, then stick A is smaller than stick C. This proposal, though, has been strongly contested by Bryant and Trabasso (1971). They found that children as young as three were able to solve such concrete transitive inference problems. They argue that the problem with Piaget's studies is that he failed to ensure that the children could remember all the relevant information. Thus, as long as they can hold the information in memory, very young children do seem able to make transitive inferences.

However, inferences in these Piagetian examples are logical inferences. The conclusion necessarily follows given the premises. But the inferences necessary to interpret the pronoun in the sentence above are not logical inferences. The conclusion does not necessarily follow given the information in the sentence. It is possible, for example, that Sue was looking for an excuse to avoid Jane, so when she had waited longer than necessary it was Sue who rushed off to get a taxi. Thus, the inferences that we make in these circumstances are plausible rather than logical.

In adult comprehension, logical inferences are certainly made during comprehension. Barclay (1973), for example, found that, in a memory test, people make transitive inferences about the spatial position of objects described in sentences and hence remember sentences that were not originally heard. But there is also a wealth of evidence that people make plausible (or pragmatic) inferences on the basis of what they read or hear. Thus, Bransford and Franks (1971) observed that people infer that unrelated sentences refer to the same individuals. More crucially, Johnson, Bransford and Solomon (1973) found that people will remember more of a sentence than was explicitly presented. That is, people make pragmatic inferences based on their general knowledge to fill out the missing elements of a sentence. Similar observations have been made by Brewer (1977).

Thus, it is clear that adults make use not only of logical inferences but also of plausible inferences based on general knowledge when comprehending sentences. It is also clear that a large proportion of pronouns that we read or hear would be uninterpretable if we did not make such plausible inferences. The question we should ask, therefore, is not just whether young children can make logical inferences but whether they can make plausible inferences to integrate what they hear into a coherent unit, and to integrate what they hear with what they already know.

The evidence for this question is somewhat scanty. It also seems to be conflicting. Some studies *have* found that young children can draw inferences from stories (e.g. Macnamara, Baker and Olson 1976, Harris 1974). However, other studies have failed to find such evidence. Both Paris and Upton (1974) and Paris and Lindauer (1976) found that children's ability to draw inferences from prose passages increased with age. However, Johnson and Smith (1981) found that third and fifth grade children (approximately eight- and ten-year olds) *could* make inferences to integrate information in passages that they read, as long as they remembered the premises. (This finding mirrors Bryant and Trabasso's (1971) finding on young children's ability to make transitive inferences.)

Johnson and Smith suggested that the major difference between the two age groups lay not in the ability to make inferences but in the range of situations that they will use for making inferences, the younger children having a much more restricted range. Such a view is compatible with Fodor's (1976) view of cognitive development. Contrary to Piaget, Fodor claims that developmental changes occur because children learn to apply innately endowed abilities to an ever increasing range of situations. However, the evidence in general for young children's use of pragmatic inferences remains equivocal. The same is true when we turn to the studies that have investigated the comprehension of pronouns.

Inferential abilities in the comprehension of pronouns

Wykes (1981) presented five-year old children with sentence pairs like the following:

Jane needed John's pencil. He gave it to her.

Jane needed Susan's pencil. She gave it to her.

In the first sentence pair, the pronouns *he* and *her* contain lexical information about gender. Hence the antecedent of *he* must be *John* and the antecedent of *her* must be *Jane*. For this sentence the pronouns can be interpreted by means of this lexical information and hence no inferences are necessary. By contrast, the second sentence pair contains two pronouns of the same gender and so they contain no lexical distinctions to constrain interpretation. Instead, the pronouns can only be interpreted by means of inferences based on general knowledge. We have to infer that if someone needs something then someone else may give that person the thing they need. Wykes asked children to act out the situations described in sentence pairs like the two above. She found virtually perfect performance for sentences pairs like the first one above. Gender information was sufficient to enable the children to interpret the pronouns correctly. However, performance was very much poorer with sentence pairs like the second one above. Young children had difficulty in using inferences to interpret the pronouns. Wykes argues that, in a control task, the children were able to make the inferences when asked explicitly to do so. The children were asked questions such as:

If John needed Susan's book, what would John do?

According to Wykes, all the children indicated by their answers that they were able to draw the relevant inferences. Hence Wykes argues that it is only when trying to interpret pronouns that children fail to use inferences. However, the control question above does not seem to query the precise inference needed to interpret the pronouns in the second sentence pair above. For those pronouns, more complex inferences seem to be required. Nevertheless, Wykes argues that five-year olds are unable to make inferences to interpret pronouns.

By contrast, Tyler (1983, Tyler and Marslen-Wilson 1982) argues that the opposite is the case. She presented children aged five, seven, and nine years, as well as adults, with sentence sets like the following:

(1) Mother saw the postman coming from a distance.
   The postman brought a letter from Uncle Charles who lives in Canada.

(2) Mother saw the postman coming from a distance.
   He brought a letter from Uncle Charles who lives in Canada.

In the experiment, the word *letter* was mispronounced *leffer*. The task for each subject was to press a key as soon as they noticed a mispronunciation: the time taken to make the key press was measured. Tyler argued that these response times are a measure of how well the mispronounced word is predictable from context. If the word is highly predictable, mispronunciations are more likely to be noticed (or will be detected more quickly). Tyler further argues that if the subjects have interpreted the pronoun in sentences like (2) above, then the word *letter* should be highly predictable – just as it is in (1). Hence subjects should be able to detect the mispronunciation with equal ease in both cases.

What Tyler found was that this was the case for all but the five-year olds. These younger children took longer to detect the mispronunciation in sentences containing pronouns – like (2) above – than in sentences containing noun phrases – like (1) above. Tyler therefore, argued that the five-year olds had not interpreted the pronoun and hence were *not* able to make use of gender information. Thus her conclusions contradict those of Wykes. Tyler also argues that five-year olds *do* use pragmatic inferences to interpret discourse and that their specific problem with pronouns is the failure to use lexical information, i.e. gender information. She bases her argument on data from two experiments. In the experiment described above, a number of different kinds of sentences were used. Example (3) shows another set from this experiment. A subsequent experiment used sets of sentences like those in example (4):

(3) Mother saw the postman coming from a distance.
    Mother brought a letter from Uncle Charles who lives in Canada.

(4) Every now and then, the princess goes to see the old shepherd.
    She takes good care of the sheep and . . .

In (3), the word *letter* was mispronounced as described above. In (4), the word *sheep* was mispronounced. Tyler found that the detection performance of all the subjects, including the five-year olds, was greatly disrupted by the implausibility of the second sentence in (3). However, only the older children and adults were affected by the implausibility of (4). The performance of the five-year olds was unaffected. Thus Tyler argues that five-year olds make inferences on the basis of general knowledge. They recognize the implausibility of (3). However, they fail to interpret the pronoun in (4), because they are unable to use the gender information. Because the pronoun is uninterpreted, they do not recognize the implausibility of (4).

The main feature of Tyler's work is its emphasis on a level of discourse representation. It is the process of updating this representation, as further sentences come in, that requires the use of inferences to integrate the new information with what has gone before. (See, for example, Haviland and Clark 1974.) The thrust of Tyler's argument is that five-year olds can make these inferences, but they cannot use lexical information to interpret pronouns. In this latter situation, inferences will not be possible. It seems, therefore, that we have two sets of conflicting results. Two points arise from this. One concerns the methodological adequacy of the experiments and the other concerns the relative contributions of linguistic (in this case, lexical) information and cognitive information (the use of pragmatic inferences) in the acquisition of pronouns.

If we consider methodology first, neither the Wykes study nor the Tyler study stands up to closer scrutiny. First, in *neither* study was the variable of pragmatic inference directly manipulated. Both studies varied only the presence or absence of gender information to manipulate whether or not pragmatic inferences were necessary. However, if we really want to test whether or not young children can interpret pronouns by means of pragmatic inferences, then we really need to vary the ease with which such inferences can be drawn. If young children do use pragmatic inferences to interpret pronouns, then they should find sentences that require simple inferences easier to understand than sentences that require complex inferences. An attempt was made to include this manipulation in a second experiment by Wykes, but the more complex inference also increased the memory load for the child, as well as complicating the task in other ways. Thus, an adequate test for children's use of inferences has yet to be made.

For instance, example (3) above seems much more obviously implausible than example (4). So using inferences to assess plausibility may well be easier in (3) than in (4). It may be for this reason that five-year olds seem more sensitive to the implausibility of (3) than of (4) and not because the children have failed to interpret the pronoun in (4). This raises a second methodological point about the studies of both Tyler and Wykes. In neither case do the sentences seem particularly suitable for five-year olds (and in Tyler's case, the detection task itself was no doubt very demanding). Wykes used sentences containing up to three pronouns and it was not always clear which pronoun caused the error. Tyler's sentences were pretested by asking the children to complete the sentences that ended just before the critical word to ensure that they did predict the critical words when the sentences were plausible. However, consistent sentence continuations may not ensure predictability of words under normal listening conditions. (See Fischler and Bloom 1979 for an example taken from reading.)

We finally need to consider the relationship between linguistic and cognitive sources of information in the acquisition of pronouns. Wykes concluded that five-year old children use lexical (gender) information *before* they are able to use pragmatic inferences. Conversely, Tyler argues that five-year olds are not able to use gender information. Hence, she suggests, they may have to rely more on pragmatic information than do older children. Clearly both linguistic and cognitive skills are developing during this period. But it remains unclear whether both are used from an early period. What is needed is a study which manipulates both linguistic complexity and pragmatic complexity. Only then can the relative contributions of the two knowledge sources be evaluated. Furthermore, a linguistic variable which manipulates Chomsky's (1981) structural constraint on pronouns would allow the relationship between general cognitive development (the use of inferences) and specific linguistic development (universal grammar) to be investigated. The fragmentary nature of the studies completed so far indicate that such an investigation is long overdue.

Children's understanding of thematic principles

One aspect of Tyler's (1983) work has not yet been commented upon. She observed that five-year olds had trouble with pronouns only when there was no obvious main character in the sets of sentences she presented. When there was a main character, then five-year olds interpreted the pronouns as easily as older children and adults. (The pronouns always referred to the main character.) Tyler interpreted this to mean that five-year olds interpret a pronoun by trying to assign it to the main character or main theme. She pointed out that such a conclusion is compatible with the work of Karmiloff-Smith (1985, 1986).

Karmiloff-Smith has analysed the speech of young children from the age of four years while telling stories from picture books. She looked particularly at the way these children used pronouns and definite and indefinite articles in their narratives. From her observations, Karmiloff-Smith proposes three levels of development. These are based on the notion that individual words have many functions. Thus, the indefinite article (*a*), for example, can be used to introduce a new entity to a listener (as in *I started a new novel yesterday*). But it also has a non-specific function where the speaker has no specific entity in mind (as in *Mary wanted to marry a millionaire*, where any old millionaire will do). Karmiloff-Smith proposes that developmental changes in behaviour reflect underlying representational changes that allow these diverse functions to be coordinated.

At level one, consisting mainly of four- and five-year olds, the children have individual representational entries for each function. So there will be an entry for *a* in its introductory use, for example, and a separate entry for *a* in its non-specific use, and separate entries for all other individual uses, regardless of whether the same word is involved, as it is in the above example. Thus the child has a large number of independent representational systems. The child is unaware that there might be any relationship between any of them, as there is in the indefinite article example.

At this level, therefore, the child is unable to coordinate his or her linguistic knowledge. The child is, therefore, very stimulus bound. New individuals are introduced into a narrative with the definite article rather than using the more usual indefinite. This is a consequence of the child being stimulus bound. He/she just says what can be seen. And what can be seen, for instance, in any particular picture is (say) *the girl*. There is no attempt to use linguistic means to indicate that the girl is a new individual in the discourse. Similarly, pronouns are only used in their deictic function. A new picture of a girl might just as easily be referred to by *she*, together with gestures, such as pointing and eye movements to indicate who they are referring to.

At level two, consisting mainly of six- and seven-year olds, there is an internal reorganization of the representational system. Individual systems come together and specific contrasts are noted, such as the use of *a* to introduce novel individuals and *the* to refer to familiar ones, or the use of *he* for masculine gender and *she* for feminine. At this stage, the child is more concerned with sorting out this newly acquired representational system than with describing the world accurately. So the child will use language very rigidly to maintain the newly acquired system of contrasts.

Here, then, the child is overconcerned with discourse constraints and will always keep the main character of the narrative in the forefront of the story. In particular, the main character will always be in the subject position and will typically be referred to by a pronoun. Thus the child is concentrating on the newly learned anaphoric use of pronouns and keeps using these pronouns to refer to the main character at the beginning of each utterance.

At level three, consisting mainly of eight- and nine-year olds, the internal reorganization that began at level two is now complete. Each word has only one entry and its different uses are noted, and the way in which each word contrasts with others is also noted explicitly. Thus, the child now has full command of the linguistic system and so is able to use language in a more flexible way than before. The child no longer sticks rigidly to the principle of referring to the main character first in an utterance and using a pronoun to do so. Instead, the child will now vary which character occupies the subject position of a sentence and will use other, more flexible, means of indicating whether the subject of the sentence is the main or a subsidiary character. If it is the main character, a pronoun will be used, as at level two. But if it is a subsidiary character, then a definite article will be used, thus providing more information about the identity of the character (i.e. *the girl* rather than *she*).

Thus, when Tyler notes that the five-year olds in her study only have difficulty with pronouns when there is no main character in the situation described by the sentences, it seems that her results are consistent with the view that her subjects are at level two and assume that pronouns always refer to the main character.

Karmiloff-Smith's account is a very ambitious attempt to *explain* how developmental changes in language development come about. Very few theories attempt this: most only describe the changes. However, the account is unlikely to be correct in its present form. Two lines of evidence suggest this conclusion. First, Clibbens (1986) found different results from Karmiloff-Smith when he changed the task. Instead of telling stories from picture books, Clibbens showed five- and seven-year old children video tapes and asked them to describe the stories they depicted. Clibbens found no evidence for a thematic subject strategy predicted by Karmiloff-Smith's level two. That is, all the children referred to both main and subsidiary characters in sentence initial position: there was no tendency to reserve the initial position of a sentence for reference to the main character.

However, the children did distinguish between main and subsidiary characters, and this effect depended on the age of the child. When a character was first mentioned, the seven-year olds used a definite noun phrase for both main and subsidiary characters. However, the five-year olds did this consistently only for the subsidiary characters. With the main characters, the five-year olds were just as likely to introduce them using a pronoun as opposed to a definite noun phrase. Thus, the five-year olds do seem to focus more carefully on the main character, but not quite in the way suggested by Karmiloff-Smith.

Such a finding, however, suggests a modification of the details of Karmiloff-Smith's view rather then a radical reconsideration and indicates that the precise formulation may well depend on the task the child is required to carry out – using picture books, which allow pointing and eye movements, or using videos which are too far away for such non-linguistic gestures to be effective.

The second line of evidence, though, is perhaps more serious. This is that the data on which Karmiloff-Smith based her theory may well give misleading information about young children's linguistic abilities. In Karmiloff-Smith's studies (and in Clibbens's study) the children were telling their stories to an experimenter who could also see the pictures (or videos). But the way a speaker refers to people or objects depends crucially on what the listener knows. Thus, if the listener already knows about an individual, a speaker will refer to that individual with a definite article. But if the individual is unknown to the listener, then the speaker will use the indefinite article to introduce the individual to the listener.

Some studies (e.g. Warden 1976) have found that young children are unable to make these adjustments. If the individual is familiar to *them* (they can see the pictures) they fail to appreciate that the individual is unfamiliar to the listener. Thus they use the definite article instead of the indefinite article the first time they mention an individual. This pattern of results is compatible with the children being at level one in Karmiloff-Smith's theory, but it has been traditionally interpreted as indicating that young children are egocentric and unable to consider the situation from the point of view of the listener.

Unfortunately, one problem with all these studies, including those of Karmiloff-Smith, is that the child is telling the stories to an experimenter who *can also see the pictures*. So, as far as the listener is concerned, the individuals *are* familiar and so the use of the definite article is, in fact, appropriate. When young children are put into a situation where the listener cannot see the pictures, then children as young as three years use the definite and indefinite articles appropriately (Emslie and Stevenson 1981). More crucially, though, for Karmiloff-Smith's theory, when children are telling stories to listeners who cannot see the pictures, their performance is *not* in accord with the three developmental levels described above. But when the same children tell stories to an experimenter who can see the pictures, then performance *is* similar to that predicted by Karmiloff-Smith's theory (Emslie 1986).

It thus seems that Karmiloff-Smith's theory provides a better account of the development of meta-linguistic awareness – the ability to reflect on knowledge of language – than of the development of early language use. For example, despite the fact that both the child and the experimenter can see the pictures, the children go through quite clear developmental stages until they speak 'as if' the experimenter could not see the pictures. Perhaps the onset of schooling facilitates this ability, and perhaps also it is facilitated by the representational changes proposed by Karmiloff-Smith. But it seems unlikely that these representational changes are responsible for very young children's early (and correct) use of both pronouns and articles.

The evidence for children's reliance on thematic principles in *early* language development is therefore not strong. It awaits an explicit test. In addition, we still need to consider the different sources of information that all have to be incorporated into a fully integrated system of communication: social, linguistic and cognitive. As yet there seem to be no studies which provide clear accounts of how the developing child brings about this integration. This is clearly a critical next step.

The present discussion suggests a number of other aspects which require further investigation. One is the need for a direct manipulation of the cognitive variable of pragmatic plausibility; second is a direct test of Karmiloff-Smith's views when applied to *early* development; third is a test of the often cited notion that deictic pronouns are acquired earlier than anaphoric pronouns (Karmiloff-Smith's data encourage the use of deictic pronouns at level one because the children can use a pronoun and point to the picture at the same time); fourth is the need for a study which investigates the relative importance of all kinds of lexical information (person, number, gender; this would also provide a test of Pinker's (1984) theory of language development); and finally an explicit test of the developmental relationship between deictic and anaphoric third person pronouns is required. There are sound theoretical reasons why deictic pronouns should appear first (no level of internal representation is required), but the data remain conflicting.

Suggested readings

Most of the work on pronouns concentrates on the linguistic aspects, and they will be covered by the suggested reading given at the end of the previous chapter. One good source is the *Papers from the Parasession on Pronouns and Anaphora*, published by the Chicago Linguistics Circle in 1980. This volume contains papers by both Karmiloff-Smith and Marslen-Wilson and Tyler. It also contains a number of other papers on pronouns and development.

CHAPTER 6

Linguistic, Cognitive and Social Factors in the Acquisition of Determiners

We will continue the discussion of the relationship between different knowledge sources by focusing now on determiners, where the syntactic constraints are minimal and the linguistic component is primarily concerned with semantics. The determiners *a* and *the* are the commonest examples of determiners. They are indefinite and definite determiners respectively.

Just as with pronouns, definite and indefinite articles can be fully used and understood only when information from different knowledge sources is combined: linguistic, conceptual and social. Linguistic information is both syntactic and semantic and we shall have more to say about this shortly. Conceptual knowledge is knowledge of objects and events in the world. For young children, this knowledge is invariably limited. The social knowledge that we will be concerned with is sometimes referred to as 'mutual knowledge' (e.g. Clark and Marshall 1981). It is basically concerned with the way people can work out what to tell a listener on the basis of what the listener already knows.

As we review the literature, we will find that the major problem for young children appears to be the limits on conceptual knowledge. The evidence is not conclusive, but it seems to suggest that from a very early age, children have mastered the semantic distinctions between *a* and *the*. They also seem to have the necessary social knowledge to base what they say on the listener's knowledge and beliefs. But the critical thing that seems to cause trouble for young children seems to be the lack of conceptual information: the knowledge of everyday objects and events and the relationships between them.

Linguistic distinctions

Syntax

As a general rule, knowledge of syntax is not a major problem for the comprehension or production of determiners. We can contrast the syntactic requirements with those of pronouns that were discussed in the last chapter. Pronouns cannot have a c-commanding antecedent in the same local domain as the pronoun. By contrast, determiners, and all other referring expressions cannot have a c-commanding antecedent even if it is not in the same local domain. Thus, in the following sentence:

He said that John liked Bill.

John cannot be co-referential with *he*, because the noun phrase *he* c-commands the referring expression *John*. Similarly, *Bill* cannot be co-referential with *he* because the noun phrase *he* c-commands *Bill* as well. The findings of Solan (1983) that were described in Chapter 4 suggest that even very young children do not interpret sentences like the one above co-referentially. It seem that the syntactic constraint places very few demands on the developing child. In fact, the aspect of linguistics that is most relevant to the use of determiners is semantics, which we will now consider.

Semantics

1. Specificity

If something is specific, a particular entity is meant, e.g. a particular chair – say the one with the broken leg – not just any chair that happens to be around. If something is non-specific, then any particular entity will do, any chair that happens to be there, for example.

From the point of view of both the listener and the speaker, if an entity is non-specific, the indefinite article is invariably used, as in

(1) Will you lend me a pencil?

Sentence (1) is an example of an indefinite noun phrase that introduces an entity into the discourse, but where the precise description of the entity is irrelevant. Any old pencil will do, both as far as the listener is concerned and as far as the speaker is concerned. We can say that an indefinite noun phrase instructs the listener to introduce a new entity into a discourse model (e.g. Johnson-Laird 1983).

If an entity is specific, then the choice of the article will depend on whether it is specific (or already familiar) to the listener or the speaker. If the entity is known to the listener, then the definite article will be used:

(2) Can you open the door?

If the entity is not known to the listener, regardless of how familiar it is to the speaker, then the indefinite article will be used:

(3) A man came to see me yesterday.

These specific uses of the articles in fact correspond quite closely to the distinction between novelty and familiarity that is described next.

2. Familiarity

Familiarity is a long standing notion in linguistics (e.g. Christopherson 1939) and it refers to a distinction between novelty and familiarity. If an entity is novel to the listener, then the indefinite article will be used. This corresponds to the use of the indefinite article for a specific entity when it is unknown, or novel, to the listener.

On the other hand, if an entity is familiar to the listener, then, *in principle*, the definite article will be used. This is not as straightforward as it sounds, and it is here that people – both speakers and listeners – can go wrong because it is necessary to make inferences about the listener's knowledge. The following is a clear instance.

(4) A man came up to me yesterday.
    He/The man was a total stranger.

By the time the listener hears the second sentence, the entity, *a man*, is familiar because it has been previously mentioned in the discourse. Hence the second mention can use a definite reference (noun phrase or pronoun). This example corresponds to the use of the definite article for a specific entity when it is known to the listener.

However, other cases are less clear. These cases are cases of 'novel definites': examples where the definite article has been used but the entity referred to has not been previously mentioned in the discourse. For example, if I ask you to close the door, I will assume that you know which door I am talking about. Normally, there is only one door in a room, so there will probably be only one entity that fits the description in the physical setting. So it will not be too hard for you to work out which door I am talking about.

On the other hand, if I say something to you about *the pub*, e.g. 'I'll meet you in the pub', then unless you are one of the small class of people that knows I always go to *The Victoria*, you may misinterpret my utterance. Alternatively, you could *infer*, from my use of the definite article, that I am talking about the pub that I go to. But that inference will not be infallible. You might infer that I am talking about an alternative pub that I once went to with you.

Class inclusion statements (or whole–part statements) are also cases of novel definites, as in the following example:

(5) I travelled by car down to London.
    The engine overheated half way there.

In this case, the use of inference is more reliable. The engine referred to in the second sentence can be inferred from the presence of a car which contains it.

There are other examples that are commonly used and easily under-stood, but which pose problems for a formal semantic account of the articles. They rely, instead, on plausible rather than logical inferences.

(6) I went to the car and opened the door.

If I am the driver, you will most probably infer that I mean the driver's door. But if I am the passenger, you will most probably infer that I mean the passenger door. So the semantics of articles are not clear cut. We can talk about specificity and we can talk about familiarity. In addition, the familiarity dimension is a complicated one and does not simply depend on whether or not the entity has been previously men-tioned in the discourse.

There have been a number of attempts to combine these two features of specificity and familiarity into a single theoretical notion: that of a discourse model or mental model. The notion of a discourse model has been proposed in artificial intelligence (Webber 1979), linguistics (Heim 1983), philosophy (Kamp 1984) and psychology (Johnson-Laird 1983). A discourse model supposes that if an entity is novel to the listener, the indefinite article, *a*, directs the listener to set up a new entity in his or her discourse model. This includes the non-specific use of *a*, where an arbitrary entity is introduced into the model. If an entity is deemed to be familiar to the listener, the speaker assumes that the listener has a unique entity in his or her model which can be referred to by *the*. The definite article is also used when there is no unique entity in the model but the speaker assumes that the listener can infer one and add it to the model.

Thus, a critical feature of discourse models is that successful communication depends on two models – the speaker's and the listener's (see e.g. Johnson-Laird and Garnham 1980). The speaker has his or her own model of the current situation and this includes a model of the listener's model. The speaker's choice of article is thus determined by what the speaker believes about the listener's model.

I will now illustrate this analysis of the articles by reviewing the literature on children's use of the articles. When examining the experimental evidence within this framework, we will conclude that young children have no difficulty with the semantics of the articles: they act as if they make use of discourse models. Young children also seem to have no difficulty with the more 'social' aspects of communication: they seem to have no difficulty working out what to say on the basis of their own and the listener's knowledge. What young children do have difficulty with is conceptual knowledge: they do not have sufficient knowledge of the world to work out what can be inferred from a novel definite. For example, a young child may not know that a car implies an engine. It may also be the case that in a number of experimental studies, the tasks that young children are required to carry out are, in fact, too difficult for them and so task difficulty alone may mask their true performance.

Experimental evidence for the specific/non-specific distinction

Three studies address the question of whether or not young children have a grasp of the specific/non-specific distinction. All three of them indicate that this distinction is grasped at a very early age. In general, young children use *the* much more frequently than *a*, so the evidence that is used shows that when children do use the indefinite article, they use it appropriately.

Brown's (1973) longitudinal study of the natural speech of Adam, Eve and Sarah found no errors at all in their speech when the entity referred to was non-specific for both the speaker and the listener. Brown concluded that by the age of roughly three years, children do control the specific/non-specific distinction as coded by the articles. Where the entity referred to was non-specific, and hence required the introduction of an arbitrary element into the listener's discourse model, the children said things like

> Put a band-aid on it. (Eve)
> This don't have a wheel on it. (Adam)
> I need a clothespin. (Adam)

These examples are shown in Table 50 of Brown (1973).

Galloway (1985) also carried out a naturalistic study of children's speech. The children were two years old at the start of the study. Her findings were very similar to Brown's. She found that the children used very few definite articles: they used mainly indefinites. These indefinites were mainly used for naming things, but the rest were invariably non-specific. Thus the children said things like:

> Make a tortoise.
> I'm using a black pencil.

Both Brown and Galloway used observational data. The only experimental study that has examined the specific/non-specific distinction is one by Maratsos (1976). Maratsos told children stories and then asked a question after each story to find out how they referred to a particular character in the story. The stories that investigated the non-specific use of *a* were ones that referred to characters in the story using *a* and that required a response to the question using *a*. An example of one of the stories is as follows:

> I know a little boy and he is very sad. He doesn't have a cat or a dog.
>
> Which does he like more?

Although both a cat and a dog are mentioned in the story, there is no reason for a specific permanent discourse entity to have been introduced into the listener's model, since according to the story no specific cat or dog exists at all. The issue of interest then, is how the children answered the final question. Did they say *the cat* (or *dog*) or did they say *a cat* (or *dog*)? The results showed that both three- and four-year old children invariably used the indefinite article. Clearly the children have not established a permanent discourse referent and have realized the need to say *a*.

This contrasts with the situation when the story says *He's got a cat and a dog* instead of *He doesn't have a cat or a dog*. After these versions of the stories, the three- and four-year olds said *the cat* (or *dog*) most of the time. The overall correct responses to these two versions of the stories were 82 per cent for the three-year olds and 99 per cent for the four-year olds. Thus, the children were able to distinguish between temporary and permanent discourse referents: a subtle and impressive performance.

These observations that young children have very little difficulty with the specific/non-specific distinction are compatible with an intriguing suggestion made by the linguist Bickerton (1984). He investigated the transition from using pidgin languages to full creole languages in communities where a number of different languages were in use. He suggested that children of pidgin speaking parents acquire a full creole language in a single generation. He used this suggestion to further propose that certain features of language are innate.

In particular, he argues that the specific/non-specific distinction is made by all children learning creole regardless of the particular mix of languages that force the use of pidgin by the parents. He suggests, for example, that when children are acquiring a creole they omit the article altogether when referring to non-specific entities, and confine their use of articles to specific entities: *a* for entities novel to the listener, *the* for entities familiar to the listener. Bickerton's work is highly speculative, (see, for example, the commentaries on his article in *Behavioural and Brain Sciences* (Bickerton 1984)). However, it is compatible with the very early use of articles to distinguish between specific and non-specific entities by English children acquiring the system of articles.

There is another line of evidence which seems to be about specificity but which I think is very difficult to interpret. In these studies, what gets manipulated is the type of referent in a visual array. I will take an example from Karmiloff-Smith (1979) to illustrate both the general features of these kinds of tasks and some of the difficulties in interpreting the data from them.

In one experiment, the visual array in front of the child consisted of two playrooms: a girl-doll's playroom and a boy-doll's playroom. The girl-doll's playroom contained:

one X	or	three X
three Y		one Y
one Z		one Z

The boy-doll's playroom contained:

three X	or	one X
one Y		three Y
one W		one W

The Xs could be distinguished by colours, otherwise they were the same.

We will call these 'similars'. The *Y*s were all identical, so mention of colour was redundant. We will call these 'identicals'. The *Z* and *W* were unique in the setting and we will call these 'singletons'. Thus, the girl-doll's playroom might consist of:

one blue book	(a singleton)
three multicoloured balls	(identicals)
one baby bottle	(a singleton)

The boy-doll's playroom might consist of:

three books (one green, one red, one yellow)	(similars)
one multicoloured ball	(a singleton)
one car	(a singleton)

The experiment required each child to play a game of 'Let's pretend'. The child was instructed to ask the boy-doll or girl-doll to lend a toy. For example, the experimenter would point to one of the toys in one of the playrooms and say to the child, *Ask the boy (girl) to lend you that*. The experimenter then recorded the nature of the children's requests, in particular, whether they used *the* for singletons, *a* for identicals, and either *a*, or *the* plus colour adjective for similars.

The major finding in this and similar studies is that up until the age of about eight years, children predominantly use the definite article for all types of object in the array. For example, when referring to one of the identicals, they just say *Lend me the ball*. Thus, they do not indicate that the ball is one of three and hence is a non-specific referent. This is a very standard finding with these kinds of experiments: children seem to overuse the definite article until very late in development.

These findings, then, seem contrary to those described above, where it was suggested that children master the non-specific use of *a* very early. However, in the experiments that manipulate the visual array for the child, the nature of the task is very different from those which observe natural speech or which rely solely on language, as in Maratsos's stories. In the array experiments, the experimenter points to the object the child must ask for, so the particular object referred to is known to both the child and the experimenter. It is not an arbitrary element at all. It might, therefore, seem perfectly reasonable for the child to refer to that object using *the*.

The task itself is also quite complicated. The child has to assume that although he or she and the experimenter share the same perceptual information, the doll – which is also physically present – does not. This requires a very complicated assessment of the experimenter's expectations in order to produce the intended correct response. It may well be that the child is not responding to the experimenter's expectations at all but to the perceptual demands of the situation. Hence, it is unclear that these experiments are manipulating specificity at all.

Furthermore, what is crucial here is that all the information is visible to all the participants in the game. So the use of non-linguistic behaviours, such as pointing or eye contact, can also be used to ensure successful communication. In fact, Maratsos (1976) noted that in a similar study, he made the children put their hands on their heads to stop them from pointing to the relevant object. More crucially, since the total array is visible to all participants, it is possible to focus on the array when describing an object. In particular, the presence of this visual array means that there is no need to use a discourse model at all to represent the entities. They are all physically present in the environment and hence are concrete and specific referents.

One of Maratsos's studies lends some support to this suggestion. He asked children to choose a toy (say a boy- or a girl-doll) when there was only one doll of each gender present or when there were three dolls of each gender. However, the critical manipulation was whether or not the dolls were visible to the child. Maratsos found that with three identical boy-dolls and three identical girl-dolls, both three- and four-year olds (the age groups tested by Maratsos) used *the* to refer to one of them when the dolls were visible. This corresponds with Karmiloff-Smith's findings.

However, when the dolls were invisible and the children could not rely on physical presence to support their communications, the same children used *a* 93 per cent of the time. These findings support the suggestion that a physically present array allows the child to identify a referent for a listener without the need to use discourse models. In fact, some additional results of Maratsos's indicate that adults produce similar results when the referents are visible as opposed to invisible to them. Thus, it seems likely that it is the presence of toys which can be seen by all participants that leads to the overuse of *the* in these experiments.

These, then, are just some of the studies that claim to explore specificity. However, I have argued that, when physical arrays are used, it may not be necessary to use linguistic knowledge at all. So the studies may not, in fact, be addressing the semantic question of specificity/non-specificity. The naturalistic data of Brown and Galloway and the story data of Maratsos are much more clear cut and favour the view that children have an early grasp of the specific/non-specific distinction. This view is compatible with Bickerton's observations that children acquiring a creole from pidgin speaking mothers spontaneously indicate the distinction by the use (or non-use) of determiners. Problems seem to arise for children when the task is so difficult that they do not know what is expected of them or when non-linguistic factors, such as pointing, help to identify what is intended to be a non-specific referent.

Experimental evidence for the novel/familiar distinction

On the surface, the evidence concerning young children's grasp of this distinction is very conflicting. The critical test has been to examine children's use of the articles when they mention a referent for the first time and then again a second time. The basic rationale is that on the first mention, the child will use an indefinite reference, because a novel entity is being introduced. However, on the second mention of the same referent, the child will use a definite (anaphoric) reference, because the referent is now familiar to the listener.

Despite this apparently simple rationale, the findings from the different studies have been contradictory. I will suggest, though, that when the results are considered from the point of view of the use of discourse models, these conflicting results become clear and can all be interpreted within this theoretical framework.

One study which examined this issue was the study of Warden (1976). He presented children between three and nine with three pictures and asked them to tell the story depicted by the pictures to the experimenter. His major finding was that when children mentioned a referent the first time, they all predominantly used the definite article instead of the indefinite one. Karmiloff-Smith (1979) obtained essentially the same findings when she asked children to describe a variety of different situations that were acted out by the experimenter. In both of these studies, the authors concluded that young children are basically egocentric: they fail to use *a* when something is known to them (from the picture or the scene), but novel to the listener. Thus they argue that young children have not mastered the novel/familiar distinction. They cannot gauge the social situation and so fail to imagine the situation from the listener's point of view.

However, these results have not been uncontested. One problem with Warden's pictures is that they are quite difficult to integrate into a single story and so the complexity of the task may have masked the children's true ability. A study by Emslie (1986) which compared the use of Warden's pictures with much simpler pictures indicated that this may well be the case. With simpler pictures, children were much more likely to use appropriate references: *a* on first mention and *the* on second mention.

A problem with the Karmiloff-Smith study is that the children gave their answers to the experimenter who had also moved the dolls. Thus, as with the array experiment, both the children and the experimenter could all see the actions and once again the linguistic demands were minimal. In order to test whether children really have mastered the familiar/novel distinction, we need a task where both the situation to be described is very simple and makes no extra cognitive demands on the child, and where the children are communicating to someone who has never seen the situation at all.

Such a study was conducted by Emslie and Stevenson (1981). They asked children aged two, three and four to tell a story described by three pictures to another child. The critical manipulations in this study were the use of very simple pictures which described a simple, straight-forward story and the requirement that the children tell their stories to other children. The lack of knowledge on the part of the listener was emphasized by the presence of a large screen between the speaker and the listener which was pointed out in the experimenter's instructions to the listener. The results of this study were clear cut. Apart from the two-year olds who primarily used naming statements, all the children used *a* when first mentioning a referent and *the* when mentioning the same referent for a second time.

These findings are what you would expect if the children were taking into account the needs and knowledge of the listener, and hence basing their communications not only on their own model of the situation but also on the listener's model of the situation. A subsequent study by Emslie (1986) made this possibility much more likely. She manipulated the knowledge or ignorance of the listener. In the 'knowledgeable' situation, the speaker described a story depicted in a short video to another child who had also watched the video. In the 'ignorant' situation, the speaker described the story to a child who was unable to see the video. The same children were used as speakers in the two situations.

The results showed that children between three and seven years were sensitive to the needs and knowledge of the listener. When the listener was knowledgeable, the speaker used *the* for both first and second mention of a referent. When the listener was ignorant, the speaker used *a* for the first mention and *the* for the second mention of a referent. Thus it seems that children's use of the articles is strongly influenced by the social situation and, in particular, by their understanding of the listener's knowledge of that situation, an observation that is compatible with the use of mental models to explain the semantic distinction between familiarity and novelty. The observation also makes explicable the overuse of *the* that was found by Karmiloff-Smith when children first mentioned a referent.

Thus it seems that children do have a grasp of semantic distinctions marked by determiners and have a good understanding of what needs to be communicated in different situations. But given these observations, we need now to ask two things:

1. Are there instances where children do fail to refer appropriately?
2. How can we explain the consistent pattern of the over use of *the* when the listener is as knowledgeable as the speaker? In particular, how can we explain the decline in this pattern as the children grow older? We have suggested that this pattern of responses is explicable if children take account of their own and their listeners' mental models. Why, then, should this pattern decline over time?

Considering question 1, there seems to be two situations where children fail to refer appropriately. One we have encountered already. This is where the cognitive demands of the task are complex enough to mask the children's true linguistic ability. This seemed to be a possibility with Karmiloff-Smith's array experiment. It also seemed to have been the case with the pictures used by Warden in his (1976) experiment. However, these can be seen as methodological blocks on performance.

A different example of where children fail to refer appropriately has a more crucial theoretical importance. This is where children have an inadequate knowledge of events and situations in the world and so fail to use a definite article to refer appropriately to a novel referent. Examples of this can be seen in an experiment by Zehler and Brewer (1982).

Zehler and Brewer asked three- and four-year olds to participate in a 'shared narrative'. With the use of toys as props, the experimenter told a story and asked the child to complete the story. They grouped the children according to both their age and their mean length of utterance to obtain four levels of linguistic ability. The conditions of interest are those that Zehler and Brewer referred to as anaphoric, context-unique and context-intermediate. In the anaphoric condition, the child was expected to complete the story by referring to an entity that had already been mentioned in the narrative.

In the context-unique condition, the child was expected to refer to an entity that could be uniquely inferred from the context of the narrative. For example, the experimenter might say *Jack went up to the door and rang?* The child was expected to continue the narrative by saying *the bell*. It is unique in that context. In the context-intermediate condition, the child was expected to refer to an entity that could be inferred, but not uniquely inferred, from the context, for example, to refer to *a* or *the door* in the context of a narrative about someone approaching a car and opening a/the door.

Zehler and Brewer found that from the third level of linguistic ability (about three years of age) children consistently use the appropriate definite articles in all three of these conditions. Below that level, it seems likely that memory limitations may have constrained the anaphoric use of *the*. The narratives were several sentences long. However, for the context-unique and the context-intermediate conditions, it seems more likely that the younger children did not have sufficient experience of the regularities of the man-made world to realize that doors normally have only one bell or to infer from the context of the narrative about a car that either the driver's door or the passenger's door was being opened. It is on the basis of this evidence that I have suggested that the real block to the development of the appropriate use of the articles is conceptual knowledge or knowledge of the world. However, while this suggestion seems reasonable, it is still in need of a specific test.

We should now consider the second question posed above. How can we explain the consistent pattern in the use of the definite article when the listener can also see the situation or set of pictures? As children grow older, their use of *the* declines, so they do start doing what the experimenter expects, rather than what would be expected if they only considered the listener's model of the physical situation. It seems that notion of a mental model of the situation cannot account for the way children use the articles in these experiments as they grow older.

The person who has done most work on the articles, and who has consistently found this developmental trend in the overuse of *the*, is Karmiloff-Smith. She has also produced a developmental model (1985) to account for this and other trends that are apparent in her data. We should consider this theoretical developmental model to see how well it can account for the data we have presented here, and also to consider it as a candidate for answering the second question we have raised.

Karmiloff-Smith's model was described in Chapter 5, so I will give only a brief recapitulation of it here. Karmiloff-Smith (1985) proposes three phases of development for articles and her model is based on the notion that each article can serve many functions. For example, the indefinite article, *a*, has a number of different functions. It can be used in naming statements, to refer to a non-specific entity (or a temporary discourse entity), and to introduce a novel entity to the listener. Thus, in phase 1, Karmiloff-Smith proposes that a child has individual lexical entries for such function, so the different functions are part of totally independent systems. It is as if each different function of *a* were really a different word which just happened to have the same sound as the other 'words' with different functions (just as the single word 'light' has at least two different meanings: light in weight and light in colour). In this phase of development the child is completely stimulus driven. They simply say what they see, hence the predominance of *the* on first mention. They see a specific object. They talk about a specific object.

In phase 2, the child's mental representation undergoes an internal reorganization. The different functional systems come together and contrasts are noted between *a* and *the*, such as the novel/familiar contrast. At this stage children are more concerned with sorting out this newly organized system than with accurately describing the world. So they become concerned with thematic discourse constraints, for example. One manifestation of this is that the subject of a sentence is always the main protagonist. It is as if the child is consolidating the inner changes at the expense of the outer world and so sticks rigidly to newly acquired discourse constraints.

In phase 3 the new internal system is fully developed. All the semantic and contextual contrasts have been acquired and mastered. So now children can consider the outer world again and modify their utterances in relation to that outer world as well as to their mental representations of the articles. One manifestation of this is that children now vary which individual is referred to in the subject position. The main protagonist is marked not by sentence position but by using a pronoun. Subsidiary characters are indicated through the use of definite noun phrases.

This analysis is an excellent attempt to account for what brings about change in behaviour during development. It is also very much in the Piagetian tradition with development being forced by an imbalance between concern about the world (phase 1) and concern about newly forming mental representations (phase 2). The major difficulty with the analysis is that the data it is based on all comes from situations where the listener is knowledgeable. So it is possible that the developmental change that is being observed has more to do with changing reactions to the social situation than with developments in the representation of the articles.

A closer inspection of Hazel Emslie's data lends some support to this position. Emslie (1986) looked at children's use of the articles when the listener was either knowledgeable or ignorant. The argument just presented would lead us to suggest that the data cited by Karmiloff-Smith will be most apparent when children are speaking to knowledgeable listeners rather than when they are speaking to ignorant listeners.

Karmiloff-Smith proposes that phase 1 children predominantly use *the* when they first mention a referent. Emslie's data indicates that this is only the case in the listener-knowledgeable condition, not in the listener-ignorant condition. Phase 2 children maintain a rigid adherence to the main protagonist, who is always placed in the subject positions. So children in this phase rarely change the subject of a sentence to refer to a different individual. Emslie's data shows that children are more likely to stick to the same subject in the listener-knowledgeable condition than in the listener-ignorant condition. So sticking to the same subject seems to have something to do with having a knowledgeable listener. In phase 3, children will change the subject, but if they do, they use a definite noun phrase not a pronoun. Emslie's data shows that children are more likely to use definite noun phrases with changed subjects in the listener-ignorant condition than in the listener-knowledgeable condition.

So, these consistent patterns of responses seem to be very dependent on the perceived state of knowledge or ignorance of the listener. Obviously, these are partly to do with the social situation (e.g. the use of *the* when both speaker and listener can see the object), and partly to do with discourse conventions: in phase 2 the main character is usually the subject; in phase 3, the main character is referred to by a pronoun and the subsidiary character by a noun phrase.

Overall, these observations suggest a number of possibilities. First, it seems that Karmiloff-Smith's analysis of the development of the articles fails to take account of the 'social' element in development. The analysis ignores the way in which young children modify their utterances according to the perceived knowledge of the listener. Second, Karmiloff-Smith concentrates on the reorganization of the child's linguistic knowledge. This can be regarded as part of the child's long-term knowledge base.

What this ignores, therefore, is the possibility of an intermediate level of representation, a discourse level representation, by which children (and adults) can keep track of the moment to moment changes in the conversational situation. We noted earlier in this chapter that, without this intermediate level of representation, it was not possible to account for the wide range of conflicting findings in this area of language development. It is this intermediate discourse level representation that emphasizes the need to consider both the child's perception of the experimental task and the child's perception of the listener's model of the situation.

Third, the findings that Karmiloff-Smith tries to account for were all obtained in situations where the child would assume that the listener (the experimenter) already had a similar mental model of the situation. Thus, her account may be describing developmental changes brought about by socialization. For example, the acquisition of what Olson calls a 'detached language' depends crucially on schooling and represents the ability of children to detach themselves from the situation and talk in the way expected of them by (say) a teacher. This idea is compatible with some of Karmiloff-Smith's own ideas about meta-linguistic awareness. It is certainly the case that she regards the acquisition of this ability as an inevitable developmental process. Thus, she may not agree that schooling is responsible for its development, and indeed her own work suggests that such an ability may develop before school age.

Whatever the final answer, two points emerge from this discussion. One is that early children's use of the articles is best explained by the notion of discourse models. It is only the introduction of this level of representation that allows a bridge to be built to link children's early semantic abilities with an understanding of common, or mutual, knowledge on the part of the listener and with the child's developing conceptual system concerning regularities in the environment.

However, Karmiloff-Smith's work suggests that there is more to development than this. She proposes that meta-linguistic awareness – the ability to detach oneself from one's language and view it analytically – must also be accounted for in a model of article usage. She accounts for this ability by proposing an alternating concentration on the world and on mental representations until the two aspects of cognition can be related at the final stage. It remains to be seen whether or not such a view can be reconciled with a view from mental models that assumes the linguistic distinctions are present right from the start.

Suggested readings

One of the best texts on the semantics of the determiners is Irena

Heim's (1983) PhD thesis. It presents an 'updated' version of the traditional familiarity view of the determiners. Karmiloff-Smith's work is also well worth looking at. In particular, her ideas on meta-linguistic awareness are much more detailed than I have described them here. A forthcoming article in *Cognition* is devoted to this topic.

CHAPTER 7

The Development of Government Binding Theory

In this chapter, I will describe in more detail the reasons for the change from the standard transformational grammar of Chomsky (1965) to the theory of government and binding of Chomsky (1981a, b). After that I will describe more fully the basic principles of government binding theory. This chapter is more technical than the previous ones! I am no longer talking about language learning but about changes in grammatical theory. It is these changes in grammatical theory that have inspired many of the ideas about language learning that I have discussed in this book.

In Chapter 2 I illustrated the model of transformational grammar which was proposed by Chomsky in 1957 and 1965. This was the model adopted as a model of acquisition at that time.

Current linguistic theory differs quite markedly from classical transformational grammar. These differences reflect not only changes in the model itself, but also changes in the way that linguists view the nature of language acquisition. In this chapter, I will discuss the changes that have been made to the model of transformational grammar itself. The issues of language acquisition is the one that has been the concern of the rest of this book.

Changes in transformational grammar

In the 1970s, standard transformational grammar went through a long transitional period. It finally emerged with a drastically reduced transformational component and enriched with a number of grammatical principles that were not present in the standard theory.

In order to describe these changes, I will return for the moment to the standard theory. I will consider certain problems for the standard theory and try to show how government binding theory overcomes these problems. Let us look again at how the standard theory treats passive sentences.

A passive sentence had the same deep structure as its related active sentence. Thus, the active sentence in (1) and the passive sentence in (2) were both derived from the deep structure shown in Figure 7.1.

(1) John kicked the ball.
(2) The ball was kicked by John.

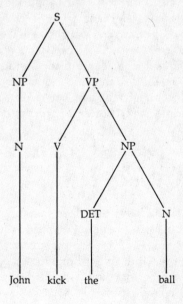

Figure 7.1

(The analysis shown in Figure 7.1 is from Chomsky 1957. For purposes of exposition, I am ignoring modifications to the passive rule that were made subsequently.) If we write out the terminal strings of the deep structure in (3), we have the following order of constituents:

	John		kick	the ball
(3) NP(1)	AUX	V	NP(2)
1	2	3	4

(AUXiliary indicates that the verb has some inflection for tense.)

The passive rule applied only to deep structures of the form shown in (3). The passive rule consisted of the following three transformations:

1. Transpose the two noun phrases (NPs).
2. Add the preposition *by*.
3. Add the auxiliary *be*.

These transformations changed the structure in (3) to that in (4):

	The ball	was	kick	by		John
	NP(2)	AUX	V			NP(1)
(4)	4	2	3	by	+	1

Thus, we could say that the passive rule applies to any deep structure with the order shown in (3) by changing the order to that shown in (4). The ordering in (3) is the *structural description* of the passive rule. That in (4) is the *structural change*. These two components, *the structural description* and the *structural change* made up the passive rule. This analysis prevents certain ungrammatical sentences from being generated. For example, the ungrammatical sentence in (5) cannot be derived from the deep structure in (3) because the ordering does not conform to that in (4):

	The ball	was	John	kick	by
	NP(2)	AUX	NP(1)	V	by
(5)	4	2	1	3

One problem, though, was that these transformational rules were very specific. Thus, the passive rule only applied to deep structures with the orderings shown in (3). If you like, the structural description pecified the context in which the passive rule could apply. Similarly, the rule of dative movement, for example, applied only to deep structures with the ordering shown in (6):

		John	give	the book	to Mary
(6) structural description:		X	V	NP	to NP
		1	2	3	4 5

The rule of dative movement changes this order to the order in (7):

	John	give	Mary	the book
(7) structural change:	X	V	NP	NP
	1	2	5	3

Thus we have a series of highly specific rules, each one applying in a particular grammatical context.

Another problem concerns the fact that some rules were optional and some were obligatory. For example, the rule of dative movement is optional. On the other hand, a transformation that forms reflexive pronouns would be obligatory. The underlying structure of *John likes John* must be converted into *John likes himself*. If this conversion did not occur, the sentence would be ungrammatical in normal contexts. So this transformation is obligatory, not optional.

The distinction between obligatory and optional rules poses a particular problem for language acquisition. First, it is a feature of transformations that varies unsystematically from rule to rule. Hence if children acquire a transformational grammar, they would have to learn this distinction separately for every rule. But how could a child learn this distinction? Suppose a child starts out with the hypothesis that all transformations are obligatory. Once the child hears sentences both with and without dative movement, this hypothesis would be disconfirmed.

However, if the child then assumes that all transformations are optional, this second hypothesis will not be disconfirmed. The child would never hear a sentence that disagreed with the hypothesis. Thus it would not be possible for a child to acquire a grammar where some transformations are obligatory and some are optional. The reason why the above hypothesis would not be disconfirmed is that negative evidence would be required to disconfirm it. For example, a child would have to produce a sentence like *John likes John* and, more crucially, be told that it was wrong. However, it seems that children are not corrected for their grammatical errors (Brown and Hanlon 1970). It is this observed lack of correction of grammatical errors that makes obligatory rules virtually impossible to acquire, if the grammar already allows optional rules. Of course, if all the rules were obligatory, there would be no problem. Similarly, if all the rules were optional, there would be no problem.

We have seen then that there are a number of problems with transformational grammar. First, it relies on a large number of specific rules, which reduces the explanatory nature of the theory. This feature additionally increases the difficulty of language acquisition. A large number of specific rules would presumably take longer to acquire than a small number of general principles. Finally, the presence of both optional and obligatory transformations poses insurmountable problems for language acquisition. In the absence of 'negative evidence', it is not certain that obligatory rules could be acquired at all.

Government binding theory

Recent work in grammatical theory goes some way towards reducing these problems. This work is the culmination of many changes in transformational grammar over the last 17 years. So the present theory is different from the standard theory in a number of ways. I will give a simplified account of these changes and try to show how, taken together, they solve the problems discussed above.

First, the structure of the model has changed. In 1965, the deep structure was both necessary and sufficient for semantic interpretation. Hence the semantic component was confined to the deep structure. It was subsequently suggested that the deep structure was necessary but not sufficient for semantic interpretation. For example, Chomsky (1971) gave examples where it was necessary to look at the surface structure as well in order to determine the meaning of a sentence. Finally, Chomsky and his co-workers (e.g. Chomsky and Lasnik 1977) proposed that deep structure (now called d-structure) was not, in fact, necessary for semantic interpretation. Instead, surface structure (now called s-structure) is both necessary and sufficient for semantic interpretation. The main reason for saying that semantic interpretation is confined to s-structures is that these s-structures now contain traces that are left behind when a transformation moves a noun phrase to a new position in the sentence. We can characterize the new model in the way shown in Figure 7.2.

We will now examine these components more closely. First of all, the phrase structure rules have been very much reduced. Instead of a list of specific rules, the phrase structure component now consists of a generalized principle derived from these rules. This principle is known as X' (pronounced X bar) syntax. So, for example, instead of rules like

VP → V NP Prep.P
PP → P NP
AP → A N
NP → DET N

there is now a single general rule of the form:

XP → . . . X . . .
(X Phrase → . . . X . . .)

or

X' → . . . X . . .

where X stands for a major lexical item such as noun, verb, adjective, preposition etc. and the dots represent lexical information that may precede or follow the major lexical item. Given this general rule, all the child has to learn is what particular categories in the language being learned stand for X, what comes in front of the X and what follows the X in a given category.

A second feature of government binding theory is the much wider range of d-structures that are generated through the X' rules. For example, active and passive sentences have different d-structures. The d-structure underlying the active sentence in (8) is (9):

(8) John kicked the ball.
(9) [[John] [kicked [the ball]]]
    S NP   VP   NP

But the d-structure underlying the passive sentence in (10) is (11):

(10) The ball was kicked by John.
(11) [[e] [was kicked [the ball] [by John]]]
    S NP VP   NP   PP

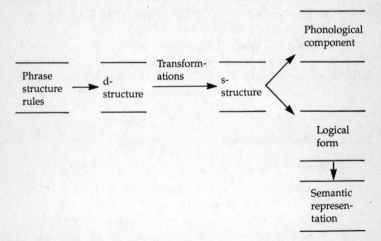

Figure 7.2

In these examples I have used a phrase structure notation in the form of brackets rather than in the form of a tree structure. The *e* in (11) stands for an empty noun phrase category.

Third, and more crucially, the role of the transformational component has been drastically reduced. No longer are there specific rearrangements of specific deep structures. Instead, a single transformational rule is assumed to apply to any deep structure whatsoever. Hence there are no insertion transformations, or substitution transformations, for example. Thus the transformational component consists of a single rule that says that any constituent can be moved to anywhere else. The application of this rule is optional in English.

Obviously, this very general rule would produce an enormous number of ungrammatical sentences. The aim of government binding theory has been to show how a small number of inter-related general principles can constrain the interpretation of sentences to account for cases where movement may occur (resulting in grammatical sentences) and where movement may not occur (because if it did the sentence would be ungrammatical).

This very general rule seems intuitively easier to learn than a grammar which consists of a set of highly specific transformational rules. All the child has to do is assume the most general rule and then learn how that rule is constrained in the language he or she learns.

This general movement rule is constrained by a set of interrelated principles which is undergoing constant revision. However, it turns out that the elements that may be moved are either NPs, as in passive constructions, or wh-phrases, as in wh-questions like *Who did you see?* I will mainly talk about NP movement.

Under certain well specified conditions, a noun phrase in a d-structure can be moved to an empty category in d-structure. This changes the word order at s-structure, but leaves a trace in the position that originally contained the noun phrase. Thus, a short passive such as

Mary was kissed.

has the following d-structure:

e was kissed Mary.

where *e* stands for an empty noun phrase category.

We have already seen that one general principle of government binding theory is case theory. Case theory claims that every lexically filled (i.e. non-empty) noun phrase must have a case assigned to it either by a verb, or by a preposition or by the feature INFL. (INFL is like inflection. It refers to verb tense and assigns case to subject nouns.) The d-structure above contains the verb *was kissed*. This means that *Mary* cannot be the object of that verb (you cannot *was kiss* someone), so *Mary* has no case assigned to it. Case theory applies a case filter in these instances which classifies such constructions as impermissible d-structures. The lexically full noun phrase (*Mary*) must have case. However, the empty category (*e*) does have a case assigned to it from the tense of the verb (i.e. from the feature INFL). Hence, the constraints of case theory force the movement of the lexically full noun phrase from a caseless position in the sentence to a cased position. This results in the following s-structure:

Mary(i) was kissed t(i).

t stands for the trace of the moved noun phrase and the bracketed letter *i* indicate that *t* and *Mary* are related.

Thus, we can say that movement is optional, but if it has not occurred, in d-structures like the one above, the resulting s-structure is marked as ungrammatical by the case filter.

Another principle of the grammar is the theta criterion. The theta criterion recognizes that every verb takes one or more arguments. For example, the verb *kiss* has two arguments: subject and object. These are interpreted as thematic roles: agent and patient. By contrast, passive verbs like *was kissed* do not take subject arguments, only object arguments (interpreted as a patient thematic role). The basic components of the theta criterion apply at the level of d-structure. They are that every overt noun phrase must be an argument of one and only one verb, and that every argument associated with a verb must be assigned. The theta criterion explains why (12) is ungrammatical:

(12) John kissed.

The object argument has not been assigned to a noun phrase, so the sentence is ruled out by the theta criterion. By contrast, the d-structure in (13) is grammatical:

(13) was kissed John.

The object argument of *was kissed* has a lexically filled noun phrase assigned to it. Naturally, the passive rule will apply to move the noun phrase from a caseless position to a cased position, resulting in the s-structure shown in (14):

(14) John(i) was kissed t(i).

The projection principle is another feature of government binding theory. The projection principle says that all the arguments of verbs are present at all levels of grammatical structure (d-structure, s-structure and logical form). The presence of the trace in the s-structure in (14) is a consequence of the projection principle: The trace fills the argument position of *was kissed*.

So far we have talked about X' syntax, case theory, the theta criterion and the projection principle. These principles apply at different levels of grammatical structure. X' syntax and the theta criterion apply to d-structures, case theory applies to s-structures. By contrast, the projection principle ensures that noun phrase arguments are available for interpretation, by the presence of *t*, even after movement has taken place.

We thus have a completely free rule of NP movement which is constrained by three general principles of grammar: the theta criterion, the case filter and the projection principle. This overcomes some of the problems of standard transformational grammar: there is only one general rule which is optional, not a series of context specific ones, only some of which are optional. There are a small number of constraints which force movement to occur if the resulting sentence is to be grammatical at both d-structure and s-structure.

However, there is yet another constraint on this free movement rule. This constraint consists of three rules of interpretation which rule out ungrammatical interpretations of sentences containing moved elements. These rules of interpretation apply to s-structures to yield permissible logical forms. Together these rules make up the principles of binding theory and they are also extremely general. They apply not only to the interpretation of traces left by moved NPs, but also to the interpretation of all other kinds of noun phrases. I will illustrate these principles by showing how sentences containing pronominal NPs and reflexive NPs are interpreted.

As a first approximation, the three rules are as follows:

1. A reflexive is bound in its governing category.
2. A pronoun is free in its governing category.
3. A definite noun phrase is free everywhere.

In 1, saying a reflexive is *bound* means that it must have a c-commanding antecedent. In 2, saying a pronoun is *free* means that it cannot have a c-commanding antecedent. Similarly, in 3, saying a noun phrase is *free* means that it cannot have a c-commanding antecedent. The difference between a pronoun and a definite noun phrase is that a pronoun cannot have a c-commanding antecedent in the same governing category (local domain), but a noun phrase cannot have a c-commanding antecedent at all, even if the potential antecedent is not in the same governing category.

These three rules of interpretation are called the *binding conditions*, and they place constraints on other kinds of noun phrases besides reflexives, pronouns and definite noun phrases. Overt noun phrases are classed into three categories: anaphors, pronominals and r-expressions. Anaphors include reflexive and reciprocal pronouns like *himself* and *each other*; pronominals include pronouns like *he*, *she*, *it*; and r-expressions ('referring' expressions) include full noun phrases like *John* or *the ball*.

The characteristics of NP traces are the same as the characteristics of anaphors. Thus, the trace in (15) is interpreted in the same way as the interpretation of reflexives.

(15) Mary(i) was kissed t(i).

The co-indexing (shown by the bracketed letter *i*) shows the grammatical interpretation.

The characteristics of null subjects are the same as the characteristics of pronominals. Thus the null subject in (16) is interpreted in the same way as a pronoun. (The null subject is called PRO.)

(16) [John(i) wants [PRO(i) to win]].

Again, the co-indexing shows the grammatical interpretation.

Finally, wh-phrases can also be moved by the movement transformation. This can be seen in (17).

(17) [Who(i) does John think [he saw t(i)]]?
     S   S

This s-structure is derived from the d-structure in (18):

(18) [John thinks [he saw who]]?
     S   S

The wh-trace in (17) has the same characteristic as an r-expression: it cannot be co-indexed with an NP in an argument position. (Wh-phrases move to non-argument positions. In (18) the arguments of both *think* and *see* have been assigned, so *who* cannot move to an argument position because that would violate the theta criterion, which says that only one noun phrase can be assigned to each argument position.)

We can now list the three principles of binding theory more accurately.

1. An anaphor is bound in its governing category.
2. A pronominal is free in its governing category.
3. An r-expression is free everywhere.

where *bound* means co-indexed with a c-commanding noun phrase, and *free* means not co-indexed with a c-commanding noun phrase.

Roughly speaking, this means that reflexives and NP traces must have an antecedent in the same governing category; pronouns and null subjects (PRO) cannot have antecedents in the same governing category; and full noun phrases and wh-traces cannot have c-commanding antecedents at all.

This was a brief account of government binding theory. We can summarize the main features as a set of interacting principles made up of:

X' theory
the movement rule
case theory
the theta criterion and thematic roles
the projection principle
the three binding conditions

It is the view of linguists working within this framework that this small set of inter-related principles is sufficient to account for the range and complexity of the languages throughout the world.

Suggested readings

Chomsky's (1981b) book *Some Concepts and Consequences of the Theory of Government and Binding* is probably the easiest source to turn to. A more detailed account can be found in his Pisa Lectures (1981a). A very understandable book has been written by Radford (1981) called *Transformational Syntax*. This was written before government binding theory was fully formed, but it gives a clear exposition of the basic principles of the theory, which is in a state of change. Chomsky's (1986) most recent book on the subject is called *Barriers* and it continues to search for a small number of general constraints ('barriers') on free movement rules.

References

Aaronson, D. and Reiber, R. (1979). *Perspectives in Psycholinguistics*. Hillsdale, NJ, Erlbaum.

Anderson, J.R. (1976). *Language, Memory and Thought*. Hillsdale, NJ, Erlbaum.

(1983). *The Architecture of Cognition*. Cambridge, MA, Harvard University Press.

(1985). *Cognitive Psychology and its Implications*, 2nd edition. New York, Freeman.

Anderson, J.R. and Bower, G.H. (1973). *Human Associative Memory*. Washington, DC, Winston.

Baker, C.L. (1979). 'Syntactic theory and the projection problem', *Linguistic Inquiry*, 10, 533–81.

Barclay, J.R. (1973). 'The role of comprehension in remembering sentences', *Cognitive Psychology*, 4, 229–54.

Barnes, S., Gutfreund, M., Satterley, D. and Wells, G. (1983). 'Characteristics of adult speech which predict children's language development', *Journal of Child Language*, 10, 65–84.

Berwick, R.C. and Weinberg, A.S. (1984). *The Grammatical Basis of Linguistic Performance*. Cambridge, MA, MIT Press.

Bever, T.G. (1970) 'The cognitive basis for linguistic structures' in J.R. Hayes (ed.), *Cognition and the Development of Language*. New York, Wiley.

Bickerton, D. (1984). 'The language bioprogram hypothesis', *Behavioral and Brain Sciences*, 7, 173–88.

Blakemore, C. (1978). 'Maturation and modification in the developing visual system' in R. Held, H.W. Leibowitz and H-L Teuber (eds), *Handbook of Sensory Physiology, vol. viii*. Berlin, Springer-Verlag.

Bowerman, M. (1982). 'Reorganizational processes in lexical and syntactic development' in E. Wanner and L.R. Gleitman (eds), *Language Acquisition: The State of the Art*. New York, Cambridge University Press.

(1983). 'How do children avoid constructing an overly general grammar in the absence of feedback about what is not a sentence?', *Papers and Reports on Child Language Development*, 22. Stanford, CA., Stanford University Department of Linguistics.

Braine, M.D.S. (1963). 'On learning the grammatical order of words', *Psychological Review*, 70, 323–48.

Braine, M.D.S. and Hardy, A.J. (1982). 'On what case categories there are, why they are, and how they develop: an amalgam of *a priori* considerations, speculation, and evidence from children' in E. Wanner and L.R. Gleitman (eds), *Language Acquisition: The State of the Art*. New York, Cambridge University Press.

Bransford, J.D. (1979). *Human Cognition: Learning, Understanding and Remembering*. Belmont, CA, Wadsworth.

Bransford, J.D. and Franks, J.J. (1971). 'The abstraction of linguistic ideas', *Cognitive Psychology*, 2, 331–50.

Brener, R. (1983). 'Learning the deictic meaning of third person pronouns', *Journal of Psycholinguistic Research*, 12, 235–62.

Bresnan, J. (1978). 'A realistic transformational grammar' in M. Halle, J. Bresnan and G. Miller (eds), *Linguistic Theory and Psychological Reality*. Cambridge, MA, MIT Press.

Brewer, W.F. (1977). 'Memory for the pragmatic implications of sentences', *Memory and Cognition*, 5, 673–8.

Brown, R. (1958). *Words and Things*, Glencoe, IL, Free Press.

(1973a). *A First Language: The Early Stages*. Cambridge, MA, Harvard University Press.

(1973b). 'Development of the first language in the human species', *American Psychologist*, 28, 97–107.

Brown, R. and Hanlon, C. (1970). 'Derivational complexity and order of acquisition in child speech' in J. Hayes (ed.), *Cognition and the Development of Language*. New York, Wiley.

Brown, R. and Herrnstein, R.J. (1975). *Psychology*. London, Methuen.

Bruner, J. (1983). *Child's Talk: Learning to Use Language*. Oxford, Oxford University Press.

Bryant, P.E. and Trabasso, T. (1971). 'Transitive inference and memory in young children', *Nature*, 232, 456–8.

Charney, R. (1980). 'Speech roles and the development of personal pronouns', *Journal of Child Language*, 7, 508–28.

Chomsky, N. (1957), *Syntactic Structures*. The Hague, Mouton.

(1965). *Aspects of the Theory of Syntax*. Cambridge, MA, MIT Press.

(1971). 'Deep structure, surface structure and semantic interpretation', in

D. Steinberg and L. Jakobovits (eds) *Semantics: An interdisciplinary Reader*. Cambridge, England, Cambridge University Press.

(1981a). *Lectures on Government and Binding*. Dordrecht, Holland, Foris Publications.

(1981b). *Some Concepts and Consequences of the Theory of Government and Binding*, Cambridge, MA, MIT Press.

(1986). *Barriers*. Cambridge, MA, MIT Press.

Chomsky, N. and Lasnik, H. (1977). 'Filters and control', *Linguistic Inquiry*, 8, 425–504.

Christopherson, P. (1939) *The Articles: A Study of Their Theory and Use in English*. Copenhagen, Einar Munksgaard.

Clark, H.H. (1979). 'Responding to indirect speech acts', *Cognitive Psychology*, 11, 430–77.

Clark, H.H. and Marshall, C.R. (1981). 'Definite reference and mutual knowledge' in A.K. Joshi, I. Sag and B. Webber (eds), *Elements of Discourse Understanding*. Cambridge, Cambridge University Press.

Clibbens, J. (1986). 'Constraints on the use of full and reduced forms of nominal reference in children's production of connected discourse' in R.A. Crawley, R.J. Stevenson and M. Tallerman (eds), *Proceedings from the Child Language Seminar 1986*. Durham University.

Deutsch, W. and Pechman, T. (1978). 'Ihr, dir, or mir? On the acquisition of pronouns in German children', *Cognition*, 6, 155–68.

Deutsch, W., Koster, C. and Koster, J. (1986). 'What can we learn from children's errors in understanding anaphora?', *Linguistics*, 24, 203–25.

Dale, P.S. (1976). *Language Development: Structure and Function*. New York, Holt, Rinehart and Winston.

Emslie, H.C. (1986), *The Development of Definite and Indefinite Articles in Young Children*. Unpublished PhD thesis, Durham University.

Emslie, H.C. and Stevenson, R.J. (1981). 'Pre-school children's use of the articles in definite and indefinite referring expressions', *Journal of Child Language*, 8, 313–28.

Fischler, I. and Bloom, P.A. (1979). 'Automatic and attentional processes in the effects of sentence contexts on word recognition', *Journal of Verbal Learning and Verbal Behaviour*, 18, 1–20.

Fodor, J.A. (1971). 'Current approaches to syntactic recognition' in D. Horton and J. Jenkins (eds), *The Perception of Language*. Columbus, OH, Merrill.

Fodor, J.A. (1976). *The Language of Thought*. Hassocks, Sussex, Harvester Press.

Forster, K.I. and Olbrei, I. (1973). 'Semantic heuristics and syntactic analysis', *Cognition*, 2, 319–47.

Frazier, L. and Fodor, J.D. (1978), 'The sausage machine: a new two stage parsing model', *Cognition*, 6, 291–325.

Galloway, C. (1985). 'The emergence of *a* and *the*: some observational data', unpublished paper, University of Lancaster.

Gleitman, L.R. and Wanner, E. (1982). 'Language acquisition: the state of the art' in E. Wanner and L.R. Gleitman (eds), *Language Acquisition: The State of the Art*. New York, Cambridge University Press.

Gold, E. (1967). 'Language identification in the limit', *Information and Control*, 16, 447–74.

Gold, G. (ed.) (1974). *The White House Transcripts*. New York, Bantam Books.

Goodluck, H. (1981). 'Children's grammar of complement subject interpretation' in S. Tavakolian (ed.), *Language Acquisition and Linguistic Theory*. Cambridge, MA, MIT Press.

(1986). 'Children's interpretation of pronouns and null NPs: an alternative view' in B. Lust (ed.), *Studies in the Acquisition of Anaphora: Defining the Constraints*. Dordrecht, Reidel Publications.

Goodluck, H. and Tavakolian, S. (1982). 'Competence and processing in children's grammar of relative clauses', *Cognition*, 11, 1–27.

Grice, P. (1975). 'Logic and conversation' in P. Cole and J.L. Morgan (eds), *Syntax and Semantics*, Volume 3: *Speech Acts*. London, New York, Academic Press.

Harris, P. (1974). 'Inferences and semantic development', *Journal of Child Language*, 2, 143–52.

Harwood, F.W. (1959). 'Quantitative study of the speech of Australian children', *Language and Speech*, 2, 236–270.

Haviland, S.E. and Clark, H.H. (1974). 'What's new? Acquiring new information as a process in comprehension', *Journal of Verbal Learning and Verbal Behaviour*, 13, 512–21.

Heim, I. (1983). *The Semantics of the Determiners*. Unpublished PhD dissertation, University of Massachusetts, Amherst.

Hsu, J.R., Cairns, H.S. and Fiengo, R.W. (1985). 'The development of grammars underlying children's interpretation of complex sentences', *Cognition*, 20, 25–48.

Johnson, H. and Smith, L.B. (1981). 'Children's inferential abilities in the context of reading to understand', *Child development*, 52, 1216–23.

Johnson, M.K., Bransford, J.D. and Solomon, S.K. (1973). 'Memory for tacit implications of sentences', *Journal of Experimental Psychology*, 98, 203–5.

Johnson-Laird, P.N. (1983). *Mental Models*. Cambridge, MA, Harvard University Press.

Johnson-Laird, P.N. and Garnham, A. (1980). 'Descriptions and discourse models', *Linguistics and Philosophy*, 3, 371–93.

Johnson-Laird, P.N. and Stevenson, R.J. (1970). 'Memory for syntax', *Nature*, 337, 412–13.

Kamp, H. (1984). 'A theory of truth and semantic representation' in J. Groenendijk, T. Jassen and M. Stokof (eds), *Truth, Interpretation and Information*, Dordrecht, Holland, Foris Publications.

Karmiloff-Smith, A. (1979). *A Functional Approach to Child Language*. Cambridge, Cambridge University Press.

(1985). 'Language and cognitive processes from a developmental perspective', *Language and Cognitive Processes*, 1, 61–85.

(1986). 'Does metalinguistic awareness have any function in language acquisition processes?' in R.A. Crawley, R.J. Stevenson and M. Tallerman (eds), *Proceedings from the Child Language Seminar, 1986*. Durham University.

(in press). 'From metaprocesses to conscious access: evidence from children's metalinguistic and repair data', *Cognition*.

Kuczaj, S.A. (1982). 'On the nature of syntactic development' in S.A. Kuczaj (ed.), *Language Development* Volume 1: *Syntax and Semantics*. Hillsdale, NJ, Erlbaum.

Limber, J. (1975). 'Unravelling competence, performance and pragmatics in the speech of young children', *Journal of Child Language*, 3, 309–18.

Lust, B. (1981). 'Constraints on anaphora in child language: a prediction for a universal' in S. Tavakolian (ed.), *Language Acquisition and Linguistic Theory*, Cambridge, MA, MIT Press.

Lyons, J. (1977). *Semantics*, Volume 2. London, Cambridge University Press.

Macnamara, U., Baker, E. and Olson, C.L. (1976). 'Four year old's understanding of pretend, forget and know: evidence for propositional operations', *Child Development*, 47, 67–70.

Maratsos, M. (1974). 'Children who get worse at understanding the passive: a replication of Bever', *Journal of Psycholinguistic Research*, 3, 65–74.

(1976). *The Use of Definite and Indefinite Reference in Young Children*. Cambridge, Cambridge University Press.

(1979). 'How to get from words to sentences' in D. Aaronson and R. Rieber (eds), *Perspectives in Psycholinguistics*. Hillsdale, NJ, Erlbaum.

(1982). 'The child's construction of grammatical categories' in E. Wanner and L.R. Gleitman (eds), *Language Acquisition: The State of the Art*. New York, Cambridge University Press.

Maratsos, M. and Abramovitch, R. (1974). 'How children understand full, truncated, and anomolous passives', *Journal of Verbal Learning and Verbal Behaviour*, 14, 145–57.

Maratsos, M. and Chalkley, M.A. (1980). 'The internal language of children's syntax: the ontogenesis and representation of syntactic categories' in K. Nelson (ed.), *Children's Language*, Volume 2. New York, Gardner Press.

Maratsos, M., Kuczaj, S.A., Fox, D.E. and Chalkley, M.A. (1979). 'Some empirical studies in the acquisition of transformational relations: passives, negatives, and the past tense' in W.A. Collins (ed.), *Minnesota Symposium on Child Psychology*, Volume 12. Hillsdale, NJ, Erlbaum.

Marcus, M.P. (1980). *A Theory of Syntactic Recognition for Natural Language*. Cambridge, MA, MIT Press.

Matthei, E.H. (1981). 'Children's interpretations of sentences containing reciprocals' in S. Tavakolian (ed.), *Language Acquisition and Linguistic Theory*, Cambridge, MA, MIT Press.

Miller, G.A. (1962). 'Some psychological studies of grammar', *American Psychologist*, 748–62.

Minsky, M. (1977). 'Frame system theory' in P.N. Johnson-Laird and P.C. Wason (eds), *Thinking: Readings in Cognitive Science*. Cambridge, Cambridge University Press.

Mohanan, K.P. (1981). 'On pronouns and their antecedents', unpublished paper, MIT (cited by Solan 1981).

Papers from the Parasession on Pronouns and Anaphora (1980). Chicago Linguistics Society, University of Chicago.

Paris, S.G. and Lindauer, B.K. (1976). 'The role of inference in children's comprehension and memory for sentences', *Cognitive Psychology*, 8, 217–27.

Paris, S.G. and Upton, L.R. (1974). 'The construction and retention of linguistic inferences by children', paper presented at the Western Psychological Association Meeting, San Francisco.

Pinker, S. (1979). 'Formal models of language learning', *Cognition*, 7, 217–83.

(1982). 'A theory of the acquisition of lexical interpretive grammars' in J. Bresnan (ed.), *The Mental Representation of Grammatical Relations*. Cambridge, MA, MIT Press.

(1984). *Language Learnability and Language Development*, Cambridge, MA, Harvard University Press.

Pinker, S., Lebeaux, D.S. and Frost, L.A. (1987). 'Productivity and constraints in the acquisition of the passive', *Cognition*, 15, 195–267.

Radford, A. (1981). *Transformational Syntax*. Cambridge, Cambridge University Press.

Reinhart, T. (1983). *Anaphora and Semantic Interpretation*, London, Croom Helm.

Rice, M.L. and Kemper, S. (1984). *Child Language and Cognition*. Baltimore, MD, University Park Press.

Richards, B. (1986). 'Yes/no questions in input and their relationship with rate of auxiliary verb development in young children' in R.A. Crawley, R.J. Stevenson and M. Tallerman (eds), *Proceedings of the Child Language Seminar*. University of Durham.

Roeper, T. and Williams, E. (eds), (1987). *Parameter Setting*. Dordrecht Reidel Publishing.

Sachs, J.S. (1967). 'Recognition memory for syntactic and semantic aspects of connected discourse', *Perception and Psychophysics*, 2, 437–42.

Schegloff, E.A. (1968). 'Sequencing in conversational openings', *American Anthropologist*, 70, 1075–95.

Schlesinger, I.M. (1977). *Production and Comprehension of Utterances*. Hillsdale, NJ, Erlbaum.

Scholes, R.J. (1981). 'Developmental comprehension of third person personal pronouns in English', *Language and Speech*, 24, 91–8.

Sheldon, A. (1974). 'The role of parallel function in the acquisition of relative clauses in English', *Journal of Verbal Learning and Verbal Behaviour*, 13, 272–81.

Slobin, D.I. (1966). 'Grammatical transformations in childhood and adult-hood', *Journal of Verbal Learning and Verbal Behaviour*, 5, 219–27.

Slobin, D.I. (1979), *Psycholinguistics*, 2nd edition. Glenview, Ill., Scott Foresman.

Snow, C.E. (1972). 'Mothers' speech to children learning language', *Child Development*, 43, 549–65.

Solan, L. (1983). *Pronominal Reference: Child Language and the Theory of Grammar*. Dordrecht, Reidel Publishing.

Stenning, K. (1978). 'Anaphora as an approach to pragmatics' in M. Halle, J. Bresnan and G.A. Miller (eds), *Linguistic Theory and Psychological Reality*. Cambridge, MA, MIT Press.

Stevenson, R.J. and Pickering, M.J. (1987). 'The effects of linguistic and non-linguistic knowledge on the acquisition of pronouns' in P. Griffiths, J. Local and A.E. Mills (eds), *Proceedings of the Child Language Seminar*, University of York.

Stevenson, R.J. and Pollitt, C. (1987). 'The acquisition of temporal terms', *Journal of Child Language*, 14, 533–45.

Strohner, H. and Nelson, K.E. (1974). 'The young child's development of sentence comprehension: influence of event probability, nonverbal context, syntactic form and strategies', *Child Development*, 45, 567–76.

Tavakolian, S.L. (1977). 'Structural principles in the acquisition of complex sentences', *Graduate Student Linguistic Association*, University of Massachusetts, Amherst.

(1978). 'Children's comprehension of pronominal subjects and missing subjects in complicated sentences' in H. Goodluck and L. Solan (eds), *Papers in the Structure and Development of Child Language*, University of Massachusetts Occasional Papers in Linguistics, Volume 4, Amherst, MA.

(1981). 'The conjoined-clause analysis of relative clauses' in S.L. Tavakolian (ed.), *Language Acquisition and Linguistic Theory*. Cambridge, MA, MIT Press.

Tyler, L.K. (1983). 'The development of discourse mapping processes: the on-line interpretation of anaphoric expressions', *Cognition*, 13, 309–41.

Tyler, L.K. and Marslen-Wilson, W.D. (1982). 'The resolution of discourse anaphors: some on-line studies', *Text*, 2, 263–91.

Wanner, E. and Gleitman, L.R. (1982). *Language Acquisition: The State of the Art*. New York, Cambridge University Press.

Warden, D. (1976). 'The influence of context on children's use of identifying expressions and references', *British Journal of Psychology*, 67, 101–12.

Webber, B.L. (1979). *A Formal approach to Discourse Ananphora*. New York, Garland.

Webster, B.O. and Ingram, D. (1972). 'The comprehension and production of the anaphoric pronouns "he", "she", "him", "her" in normal and linguistically deviant children: a preliminary report', *Papers and Reports on Child Language Development*, 4, Stanford University.

Wykes, T. (1981). 'Inference and children's comprehension of pronouns', *Journal of Experimental Child Psychology*, 32, 264–78.

Zehler, A.M. and Brewer, W.F. (1982). 'Sequence and principles in article system use: an examination of *a*, *the* and *null* acquisition', *Child Development*, 53, 1268–74.

Author Index

Subject Index